FROM
HERE

ALSO BY LUMA MUFLEH

*Learning America: One Woman's Fight for
Educational Justice for Refugee Children*

FROM HERE

A MEMOIR
LUMA MUFLEH

NANCY PAULSEN BOOKS

NANCY PAULSEN BOOKS

An imprint of Penguin Random House LLC, New York

First published in the United States of America by Nancy Paulsen Books,
an imprint of Penguin Random House LLC, 2023

Nancy Paulsen Books & colophon are trademarks of Penguin Random House LLC.
The Penguin colophon is a registered trademark of Penguin Books Limited.

Visit us online at penguinrandomhouse.com.

Library of Congress Cataloging-in-Publication Data
Names: Mufleh, Luma, author.
Title: From here: a memoir / Luma Mufleh.
Description: New York: Nancy Paulsen Books, 2023. | Summary: "Refugee advocate
Luma Mufleh writes of her tumultuous journey to reconcile her identity as a gay Muslim
woman and a proud Arab-turned-American refugee"—Provided by publisher.
Identifiers: LCCN 2022053881 (print) | LCCN 2022053882 (ebook) |
ISBN 9780593354452 (hardcover) | ISBN 9780593354469 (ebook)
Subjects: LCSH: Mufleh, Luma—Juvenile literature. | Refugees, Arab—United States—
Biography—Juvenile literature. | Muslim lesbians—Biography—Juvenile literature. |
Sexual minority political refugees—United States—Biography—Juvenile literature.
Classification: LCC HV640.5.A6 M84 2023 (print) | LCC HV640.5.A6 (ebook) |
DDC 305.9/06914089927073 [B]—dc23/eng/20221207
LC record available at https://lccn.loc.gov/2022053881
LC ebook record available at https://lccn.loc.gov/2022053882

Printed in the United States of America
ISBN 9780593354452
1   3   5   7   9   10   8   6   4   2
BVG

Edited by Stacey Barney | Design by Suki Boynton | Text set in Maxime Pro

This is a work of nonfiction. Some names and identifying details have been changed.

For Zeina and Yazan (Leila, you got your own chapter!)
and for all the black sheep, you are the G.O.A.T.

FROM
HERE

PROLOGUE
A QUESTION

"IS YOUR DAD dead?"

Leila doesn't make eye contact. Her five-year-old legs stretch out over mine. We're still in pajamas, our labneh-smeared plates stacked by the sink. The kitchen floor beneath us is cold after a long winter. Her question is a gut-punch.

"No." I clear my throat and turn her face to mine. "Why would you ask me that?"

"Because we only talk to Taytay and Namo and Khalo," she says, meaning her grandmother, aunt, and uncles.

"We just don't talk to each other," I offer, already knowing it won't be enough.

"Why?"

Emily had warned me this might happen. Leila had been asking questions, she said, maybe I should be ready for them. But how do you tell your daughter that some families, in fact, disown their daughters? That mine did it twice? That you can still love a country even when it does not love you back?

If there are answers to these questions, I don't know them. So I go with something simple. "Because he doesn't understand me." I work my fingers through her hair, tangled from the kind of deep sleep I must have had once. "He doesn't like that I married Mommy."

"Why doesn't he like Mommy? Everyone loves Mommy." Leila's eyes narrow like she's ready for a fight. I've said the wrong thing.

"In Jordan, two women can't get married."

"What would happen to you?"

"I'd probably be killed."

"But you said Jordan is beautiful!"

"It is beautiful, Leiloushti."

Leila goes quiet. Next to us, my phone is dark. I imagine my mother in Amman, waiting by her own phone, halos of cigarette smoke around her sunny-brown hair. It's been half a dozen years since she and my father moved from the palatial estate of my childhood and into an apartment nearby, more appropriate for the two of them and their small staff. I will likely never see the room that she waits in for our calls, but I can picture her fussed-over houseplants, the throbbing reds and blues of the Persian rug at her feet.

I think about what Leila knows: about the time my cousin Omar and I drank the "magic potions" we made from our uncle's chemistry set, how my grandmother rushed us to the hospital so quickly she forgot to put on her hijab. I've told her about sneaking the car out when I was eight years old and crashing it into a tree. I've explained all the Muslim holidays to her, the best pastries for Eid, what it's like to float in the Dead Sea. She's learned how to cook using her nose. She's heard about the soccer games in the streets, about the two tortoises we used for goalposts and how they would wander off midgame. She knows about the pistachio rolled ice cream that I ate with my cousins during Amman's endless summers.

I think about what Leila doesn't know: The suicide attempts. The policeman pointing a gun at the back of my head. My first sexual experience, a terrible secret with a much older woman. The honor killings. The asylum hearings and weeks spent alone and shivering on a Greyhound bus. Emily's and my wedding, when not a single member of my family showed up. All the years I would call home, only to hear the click of the dial tone. The parts of my story I've left out to protect my daughter's innocence, the version of the world I would like her to live in.

I take a deep breath.

"Do you want to talk to Jiddo?"

Leila's body stiffens against mine. She calls my bluff. She doesn't even hesitate. "Yes!" she says with the enviable confidence of a child. I don't want to stand in the way of her getting to know her grandfather. I want her to believe that all people are good. I want to believe the same thing.

TECHNICALLY, THE LAST time I spoke to my father was seven years before that morning on the kitchen floor. Before Leila, before the new house and school in Columbus. In many ways my father and I were strangers to each other even then, still navigating a tense reconciliation after our first seven years of silence.

I asked Emily to marry me in Illinois, conspiring with her family to surprise her. Her sister scattered Ring Pops—I had always threatened to propose with one—like rose petals along the sidewalk that led to Emily's favorite breakfast joint. It was a Midwestern April, bright and wet. The ground soaked through the knee of my pants; the sun burned my eyes as I looked up at her.

"Did you say yes?" I asked, practically panting, my face pressed against Emily's shoulder.

"Did you ask anything?" she teased. I didn't know if I had.

The restaurant was full of relatives and friends—when Emily saw them, she put her hands over her heart, her curls swung with wild laughter. We collected hugs and clinked glasses and reveled in the hours made, it seemed, just for us. Even her divorced parents set aside old resentments for the morning. Looking at them, I wondered how I could be so good at mending other people's families, but never mine. Amid so much joy, that familiar loneliness found me; all I could see were empty chairs where my own family should have been.

Later, in the quiet of her mother's guest bedroom, Emily wanted to know if I had told my parents about our engagement yet. "You always think worst-case scenario," she said. I didn't know how to tell her that the scenarios I thought about were so much worse now that her feelings were at stake.

In the email to my parents the next day, I wrote, *I know this is hard for you to hear, because this is not what you expected for your daughter. But I have never been happier, and I hope I can have your blessings.*

Even though I also wrote, *I haven't told anyone else in the family—I want to share it with you first,* it was my brother who called a few days later, after Emily and I had returned home to Atlanta.

"How could you do this?" he asked, and I wondered which part he thought was more audacious: that I had fallen in love or that I expected anybody to be happy for me. "Couldn't you wait until they died?"

"Until they died? Seriously, Ali? That's the best you've got?" I raged at him. I smacked the steering wheel of my parked car, baking in the Georgia sun.

"*And* she's Jewish!"

"Jews and Muslims have a lot in common. We don't eat pig—"

"This is not funny."

"It is a little funny," I taunted.

"Why are you doing this?"

"The same reason you did it. We're in love. We're going to have kids."

"Kids? Are you crazy? You can't have kids."

"Why? Because she's a woman? Or because she's Jewish?"

"Just don't expect them to call you," he warned.

"Kul kharah," I told him. *Eat shit.*

We hung up on each other.

Months later, in a hotel room in California, where Emily and I were looking at wedding venues, my mother's number appeared on my cell phone.

"Answer it!" Emily urged, a wellspring of hope. She perched on the edge of the bed during the call, smiling and searching my eyes as if they might translate Arabic into something she could understand.

"Well! What did she say?"

"She said that it's hot there."

My mother continued to call me to report on the weather, a heat wave or a cloudy day. Before the wedding, and after. After Leila was born, then Zeina, then Yazan. When the girls were old enough, we began our Saturday morning video chats. She never mentioned the email. Looking back now, I can see that her phone calls were her way of being there for me in the only way she knew how. Those mundane calls were a radical defiance. She was still there.

My father never responded.

MY MOTHER'S SATURDAY is seven hours ahead of ours. She looks elegant as always, and I'm sure the tag in her shirt says *dry clean only*. I try not to glance at my own tiny portrait in the corner of the screen. My T-shirt. My disheveled hair. I know my mother won't say anything; she doesn't need to.

"Mama, is Baba there?"

"Seriously?" A wide Syrian smile spreads across my mother's face.

"Yes, get Baba."

She is replaced by a tilted view of the ceiling. I give Leila a squeeze. She bounces in excitement. Emily is nearby. I can feel her listening. A commotion of light flashes across the screen, and then my father's face materializes in my outstretched hand. My mother's after that.

I have seen pictures of him during the silence. When my mom or sister sends photos of vacations, family gatherings, or weddings, sometimes my father's face appears in them like a phantom. It has always made me feel numb, as if I am looking at a person I have met but whose name I don't remember. Now, before me, I can see how much older he has gotten. Thinner, though, maybe even healthier. There's a new beard. I'm not sure how I feel about it.

"Baba, this is Leila—"

"I'm Leila!" she interjects. I don't know if she is rescuing me or simply unable to restrain herself. I move my face out of frame.

"I know! Hello, Leila!"

The three of them gaze at one another for long, happy seconds.

"I have a brother and a sister," she announces.

"I know, habibti." I search my memory for a smile this big on my father's face. I turn up nothing.

"Today we are going to the park, and maybe swimming."

"You know how to swim?"

"Yes, Mama taught me and Zeina how to swim. We love to swim. Do you know how to swim?"

"Yes, I like to swim."

My chest is tight, and my throat is dry. "Okay, we have to go now," I manage with what I hope might pass as a cheerful tone.

When the screen goes dark, Leila, satisfied, jumps off my lap, ready to find her younger sister and share the happy news—they have another grandpa.

"Are you okay?" Emily asks. She's tucking chairs under the kitchen table.

"I'm fine." If anyone knows about my powers of compartmentalization, it's Emily. "Time to get ready! Socks and shoes! Who wants cinnamon rolls?"

Both girls appear in the doorway, each trying to be louder than the other: "I do!"

"How many cinnamon rolls today, Zeina?"

"Forty-four." She grins, ready for our game.

"How about one *hundred* and forty-four?" Zeina is becoming something of a folk hero in our neighborhood, downing huge cinnamon rolls like mere dinner mints.

We gather jackets, wrestle with the stroller. A few minutes later we are a brigade of sneakers and mismatched socks, marching to the bakery. I try to forget my father's face, to push it down deep and hide it, like I always do. I try to tuck the past away in its assigned compartment and rejoin the present moment. But as we walk, my mind is racing, and I know that, at some point, I will have to tell Leila everything. She will never truly understand herself if she doesn't know her family's history and the complexity of her identity. If she does not know about the scars, the strength, and resiliency she has inherited.

As I watch my children wolf down their pastries, I am overwhelmed with all the things I need to tell them. What has shaped me and what has saved me, and how I found purpose, belonging, and home in the most unexpected places.

This is what I want them to know.

PART I

CHAPTER 1
TOM

I WAS LEILA'S age the first time I watched a sheep get slaughtered.

It was Eid al-Adha, the holiday that celebrates Abraham's willingness to sacrifice his son to prove his devotion to God. At the last minute, God intervened and provided Abraham a sheep to kill instead. On Eid al-Adha, Muslims celebrate Abraham's unwavering faith and God's mercy by slaughtering an animal—usually a goat or a sheep—and sharing the meat with relatives, neighbors, and the poor.

At six years old, I knew the story of Abraham; sometimes I'd scare my younger brother Ali by saying, "Imagine if God didn't stop him—you'd be dead." But for me, the holiday was about something much more important: new clothes and money. For Muslim children, Eid al-Adha is one of the best weeks of the year. No school, new outfits, and at the end of the week, the toy stores open back up for kids to spend their Eid money on various treasures: a soccer ball, water guns, comic books, and Pop Rocks.

That year, we celebrated Eid al-Adha with my dad's side of the family. We called my dad's father Jiddo Riyad (Grandpa Riyad), and his house was in the same neighborhood as ours. We lived in Amman, the capital of Jordan. Amman was built across seven hills, or jabals, and each hill was its own neighborhood. Our neighborhood, Jabal Amman, was well-known for being where the royal family and prime minister lived. Jiddo Riyad's house was across the street from the Qatar embassy. The British, French, and Spanish consulates were just down the road. Because the neighborhood was full of royalty and diplomats, a Jordanian soldier was stationed outside many of the homes, including Jiddo Riyad's. They wore blue berets and held rifles.

Jiddo Riyad's house stood like a fort behind a concrete wall, snaking out in all directions, full of dark rooms I had never seen. It had to be a big house because my grandfather had thirteen kids, six boys and seven girls, and among them they had dozens of their own children. I grew up in a legion of cousins, and on holidays like Eid al-Adha, all of us (almost without exception) gathered at Jiddo Riyad's to celebrate. It was roomy enough for everyone, and modern enough to be comfortable—except for one bathroom that still featured a squat toilet, a porcelain bowl sunk into the floor that required much balance and care. Even though his children complained, my grandfather made a point of keeping this old-world fixture. Jiddo Riyad came from a very old village called Salt. Maybe because of this, he sometimes seemed uncomfortable with fancy things; it was important to him to hold on to the customs and traditions of his youth.

For most of the day we would play outside, usually never-ending games of soccer, but also plucking nuts from the pistachio trees and scrambling around the large fountain that was always mysteriously dry. Behind the house and down a set of stone steps, a metal playground gleamed in the desert sun, complete with a seesaw, a slide, swings, and monkey bars. By late morning the slide would be so searingly hot that we'd have to use old rice sacks to protect our skin from burns.

The most exciting part of Eid was when Jiddo Riyad would summon each grandchild to his recliner, where he would dole out money to us, one by one. An imposing man despite his white hair and short stature, Jiddo Riyad's steel factories had made him a millionaire and quite prominent in Amman. He was feared and respected in his own family and throughout the city. Normally he was serious and reserved, but handing out gifts to his grandchildren made him glow with delight. Because I was the oldest child in my family, and the oldest grandchild of Jiddo Riyad's second wife, I often received more money than my cousins. It was my responsibility to care for my younger siblings, and many years I would organize a pool between us, so we could afford a more valuable gift from the toy store, something we could share.

After the money was handed out, we would assemble in the family dining room for a feast of mansaf, lamb simmered in yogurt and served over rice. Mansaf is not only my favorite meal, but also the national dish of Jordan. It is served on the holiest days of the Muslim calendar and has been used for centuries as peace offerings between tribes. Mansaf is always served from a massive communal dish and eaten with the hands. When we ate mansaf, we didn't sit at the table, we stood around it, sleeves rolled up, reaching into the platter for fistfuls of rice. The meat served on Eid al-Adha comes from the animal that has been sacrificed that day, and each year my grandfather hired men to slaughter thirteen sheep for his thirteen children. Most families only sacrifice a lamb for every son, just as Abraham did. But because our family was so well-off, it was expected that we would distribute a greater amount of meat to the poor.

I had never given much thought to the lamb in our mansaf, until that year, the year I turned seven, and my cousin Hussein suggested we go watch the men as they performed the ritual. Hussein was four years older than the group of cousins I tended to play with, confident and cocky. I didn't really want to watch whatever happened outside, but I didn't want Hussein to think I was scared either. I took my younger brother Ali by the hand, and together we followed Hussein to the backyard.

We chose the flat, elevated area, a spot where we normally played cards or marbles. From there we were only about ten feet from the playground, where three men were sharpening long, swordlike knives. They were dressed in loose-fitting gray linen and wore kaffiyehs, the traditional Arab headdress. Behind them, a pack of dirty white sheep stood together in a line, looking oblivious.

"So they'll slit the throat, and you'll see all this blood drain," said Hussein with annoying authority. I could tell now that he had brought us here simply to show off how smart and tough he thought he was. "And the sheep will kick and make these crying noises, and then they'll hang it upside down on the hook, and all the blood will come out, and then the sheep will stop making noises and die. It's not scary, just watch."

I squeezed Ali. He was only five, his dark hair trimmed into a perfect bowl cut. "Get ready to close your eyes," I whispered. I didn't want him to embarrass us in front of Hussein. "Whatever you do, don't scream." I kept my hands on his shoulders so that I could cover his mouth if he did.

Below us, the men clinked their knives together and prayed in unison. As two of the men sandwiched the first sheep between their legs, I took a deep breath. The man in the front pulled the animal's head back and in one sharp motion drew his knife across its neck. Just as Hussein had promised, a curtain of blood poured from the wound, instantly soaking the dusty ground and the bottom of the men's pants. As the sheep shuddered and groaned, the second man quickly wrapped a rope around its back legs and flipped it upside down. With little struggle, he hung the animal on an S-shaped hook that was dangling from the monkey bars. For a few long seconds, it kicked and screeched and swung chaotically, blood raining down everywhere, creating dark pools in the dirt. Then all at once, it went silent and still, and the men bowed their heads in prayer.

It was as if my mouth and throat had been stuffed with wool. We weren't supposed to pray when we were dirty, I knew that. And we weren't supposed to kill things or hurt them either. Everything that was happening in front of me was wrong. I let go of Ali's shoulders and pushed past Hussein. I knew the men would not question me; they were my grandfather's employees. I marched past the swings and the slide and snatched the rope of the first sheep I came to.

"What are you doing?" I heard Hussein yell behind me.

"This one's mine. I'm taking it," I shouted back.

"Where are you taking it?"

"They are not going to kill my sheep. I'm taking it inside Jiddo's house. It can live there."

"Put it back before you get in trouble!"

"No!"

The sheep followed without protest as I led it toward

the house. I knew I couldn't walk into the dining room with it; all of the adults were gathered there. Instead, I made my way to the door that we almost never used, the one that opened to Jiddo Riyad's formal living room, a space reserved solely for entertaining important guests—not for children and certainly not for sheep. Inside, red and black rugs were layered over the concrete floor, filling the room with a raw and dusty smell. Shafts of midafternoon sunlight took aim through the windows, and plush cushions sat ready for visitors. I threw myself down on one of them.

For the first time, I looked at the sheep, now at eye level. "It's going to be okay," I told it. I petted its tangled, wiry coat.

Hussein and Ali were the first to arrive. But soon, more cousins streamed in. Then my father was there; my mother, too.

"Luma!" my father said. "What is going on?"

"There was blood everywhere! They can't kill this sheep," I argued. "It's mine."

"You need to take the sheep outside right now. Jiddo will not be okay with this." Next to him, my mother, a strict vegetarian, stood with her arms crossed in a show of solidarity with my dad, but I swear I saw a smirk pass over her lips.

"What's going on?" My grandfather's voice came from the door.

My father stepped out of Jiddo's way. Everyone always stepped out of Jiddo's way.

"Jiddo, I know we are supposed to kill sheep for Eid. But

you cannot kill . . . Tom." Perhaps if the sheep had a name, I reasoned, Jiddo Riyad would be less likely to slaughter it. The only animals I knew were the ones on TV, and at the time, *Tom and Jerry* was my favorite cartoon.

"Tom?" Jiddo Riyad repeated, looking confused. My grandfather rarely spoke English; the Western name sounded weird coming from his mouth.

"Yes, this is Tom, and I don't want him to die. There are enough sheep we are killing today, and I love Tom. You have a big house; he can live here with you." I wondered: could a sheep use a squat toilet?

The room seemed to fill with a thick tension—like a balloon about to burst—as everyone waited for Jiddo Riyad to reprimand me. Out of the corner of my eye, I saw Hussein put his hand over his mouth. My father shook his head in shame. My mother said nothing.

And then Jiddo Riyad did something no one expected him to do. He laughed. His laughter seemed to give everyone else permission to do the same.

"Okay, we will keep Tom," he said to me, and then, to my father: "You have your hands full with this one."

As the adults filed out, my cousins gathered around Tom and me, laughing and petting the lucky sheep.

WHEN IT WAS time to eat, I left Tom in the living room, satisfied that he would be safe and comfortable while we ate the family meal. (I know now that my grandfather let Tom stay for a few days. What happened to him afterward I can only imagine.) When the platter of mansaf was placed at the kids' table, we stood around and scooped rice with our hands. Every time I reached for the lamb, though, my cousins would push the plate just out of reach.

"What are you doing?" I asked, irritated.

"You can't eat Jerry!" Hussein said with a haughty sneer. The rest of my cousins giggled.

"You're a jerk," I said.

"Luma, come here." Jiddo Riyad beckoned from the adult table. "Come stand next to me."

The invitation surprised me. My grandfather always stood at the head of the table; whoever was invited to eat next to him was considered the guest of honor; typically it was a person about to graduate or get married. Even at seven years old, I understood how meaningful Jiddo Riyad's gesture was.

"Yes, Jiddo," I said obediently.

Jiddo Riyad gathered me in the crook of his arm. With his other hand he formed a small ball of rice and lovingly placed it near my lips. I smiled and took a bite. I hoped Hussein was watching.

"Here," Jiddo said, reaching for one of the lamb bones. He was offering me the marrow, the delicacy the adults usually argued over. My cousins had tried marrow; they said it was gross. Sure enough, it looked oily and brown, like spoiled pudding. But now, with all eyes on me, my revered grandfather holding me affectionately, what *felt* right and what *was* right seemed very far apart. I didn't want to eat one of those innocent animals that had died on the playground, but I was hungry, and I didn't want to disappoint my family.

I tipped my head back and sucked the marrow straight from the bone.

CHAPTER 2
BOMBS ABOUT TO EXPLODE

MY OTHER SET of grandparents also lived in Jabal Amman, a short walk in the opposite direction. The time we spent there looked similar—backyard soccer games and large family meals—but felt very different. Their house was smaller in a cozy way, louder in a laid-back way. For much of my childhood it was my favorite place to be.

My grandmother's name was Munawar, the Arabic word for "illuminated" or "bright light." It was the perfect name for her. Her hazel eyes shone, and her pink cheeks glowed, and she seemed to emit a kind of warmth that I only ever felt in her home, in her presence. Her siblings called her Noura for short, and I called her Taytay, Grandmother.

Taytay was pure affection. Her embraces were the full-body kind. She had a massive sectional couch that snaked around her living room, big enough for her six children and their children, too. When you sat next to Taytay, she would rub your back or scratch your head. This was very different from family time at Jiddo Riyad's house, where my grandfather's recliner presided over two rows of seating, almost like a king holding court. When Jiddo Riyad was watching TV, no one dared to speak. When the TV was on at Taytay's house, you couldn't hear it over the laughter.

Like Jiddo Riyad, Taytay was a devout Muslim, but she did things her own way. She wore a hijab, the traditional head covering for Muslim women, but also left a few strands of her brown hair revealed. While many Muslim women shrouded their entire bodies, Taytay wore her clothes to the elbow and the knee. Sometimes I would ask her why she didn't cover up head to toe like the others. She would laugh and remind me that we lived in the desert. The Quran required us to be modest, not stupid.

The Quran *was* very explicit that we should pray five times a day, facing the holy city of Mecca, and performing salat, dropping to our knees and putting our foreheads on the ground. When my cousins warned me that I would have to make up every prayer I missed on the floor of hell, I came to Taytay upset and scared. I was a typical kid; I tried to stick with it, but there was always something more fun or interesting to do than pray. I had skipped so many prayers that my forehead would be burnt to a crisp.

"Do you think Allah would ever harm you like that?" she assured me. "Allah is merciful and compassionate."

Relieved, I thought of another one of my cousins' threats. "What about if we don't finish our food? Will we have to eat it before we are allowed in heaven?"

At this, she grinned. "Only the eggplant will follow you."

My hatred of eggplant was an affront to Taytay, who baked it, pickled it, put it in stews, and grilled it with garlic-yogurt sauce. Taytay's Islam was peaceful and kind—except when it came to eggplant.

I shared Taytay with my two younger brothers, Ali and Saeed, and an ever-growing number of cousins. Sometimes, though, I got very lucky and had her all to myself. I would help her in the garden, where she grew a whole market's worth of food: apricots and grapes, tomatoes and big bunches of parsley. She even managed to coax cherry and sour plum trees from the ground. Her flower beds overflowed with the colors of her cherished Syria: red roses, white jasmine, and purple wisteria.

Other times I would sit on the counter while she cooked, which she did almost entirely by smell; there were no cup or tablespoon measures in Taytay's kitchen. Instead, she would lean over the pot, scowling in concentration. When the right spice combination hit her nostrils, she would raise her head and smile, nodding approvingly. On the best afternoons, she made kibbeh, football-shaped dumplings of ground lamb fried in a crispy shell of bulgur wheat.

"Like this, Lamloom," she would say as she modeled

how to mold the wheat into a vessel for the meat. But it was no use; my clumsy hands couldn't make the same motions. My kibbeh balls were always lopsided or torn. Instead of stuffing them with lamb, Taytay would have me roll a little baton of wheat to accompany my empty kibbeh, which she would fry until they were golden and crunchy, and then present at dinner on their own plate. We called them duu do, Arabic for "knock knock," because of the way they looked like a mortar and pestle. We had our own language for lots of things.

When I was old enough to be helpful, around eight or nine years old, Taytay started taking me to the market. On those days, we would climb into the boxy green Mercedes she kept parked under the grape trellis. Despite the shade the trellis provided, the leather interior of the car was always nuclear-hot, and I'd sit low in my seat to avoid burning the back of my thighs.

The markets were outside, with rows of produce vendors lined up along a narrow path of dusty concrete. Around one corner was the bakery where we bought our fresh pita; around the other was the butcher. There were bags of rice as tall as me and bags of spices rolled open to reveal their vibrant colors and scents. Some of the fruit stands were operated by kids my age; most were run by older men with serious faces. They shouted over each other as they restocked their shelves: "Eggplants!" "Tomatoes!"

"Lemons!" "Ten for a JD!" If you didn't speak Arabic, you would think they were fighting.

If it was especially busy and no one would come to the car to assist us, Taytay would send me into the market on my own and I would use my small body to weave through the throngs of shoppers. Other times we would walk together to our reliable grocers, the men we could count on to have the very best produce. I loved watching Taytay barter and charm, the way she knew when to push and when to walk away. The way she knew which vendors hid the good stuff in the back—Egyptian mangos, sugar apples, and loquats. The way she would use her magic nostrils to tell how good the fruit was.

Once everything was loaded into the cavernous trunk of the Mercedes, we would head home, keeping the sour green plums in the front seat between us. We always had the fruit man salt the plums, our reward for getting the shopping done.

OUR LIFE WAS good. Full of family and food and trips to the beautiful places near our home. But it wasn't always that way for my mother and her parents. They weren't Jordanian; they were from Damascus, the capital of Syria.

In 1964, a decade before I was born, the Ba'ath Party had taken control of the Syrian government, along with everything else in the country: the military, the banks, the schools, and the factories. They said that the government would take care of everyone equally. They said that this was how Syria would achieve unity. But their version of equality and unity was not optional—it was mandatory. Anyone who didn't comply was thrown in jail, tortured, or killed. The brutality of the regime would change Syria forever.

As the owner of a clothing factory that employed hundreds of people, my grandfather was targeted by the leaders of the new regime. Soldiers waited for him at his work and at the mosque, eager to jail him because he refused to hand over his factory to the government.

Like many families in Damascus, my grandparents lived in a three-story courtyard apartment building, full of uncles, aunts, and cousins. To evade capture, Jiddo Suheil began spending each night in a different unit with a different family member, rarely sleeping, mostly praying and waiting for the knock on the door.

It was my grandmother who left first. Unwilling to live in harm's way any longer and six months pregnant, she loaded her five children into the family car and drove 128 miles from their old life in Damascus—their friends, family, and schools—to find safety in Amman. From the front seat, my sixteen-year-old mother sobbed as the orchards and pine groves of Syria gave way to the dusty hills of Jordan. They were refugees. After two of his brothers were arrested and his factory finally seized, Jiddo Suheil accepted that if he didn't leave his beloved country, he would certainly die there. The Syria he knew was no more.

They lost so much. The brothers who were tortured and killed. The factory and the life savings. Most of all, my grandparents lost their country, their history, and their culture. The big things like the family heirlooms and photographs, and the little things like the smell of cherry trees, Friday night picnics, and family outings to the mountains or the Mediterranean coast. A community they were a part of and a sense of belonging that comes from being born in a place and staying there. They no longer had a place to call home.

Even though Jordan and Syria share a border, they are very different countries. Different accents, different skin tones, different facial features. Syrian food was elaborate and light; Jordanian cuisine was basic and heavy. Syrian culture was urbane and cosmopolitan; Jordan didn't even have a university until 1962. Syrian people were well educated and quick to adapt; Jordanians resented the influx of capable foreigners into their country.

My grandparents were outsiders in Jordan, and their light eyes and soft, singsong Syrian accents gave them away. Still, they persevered. Grateful to Jordan for taking them in, they created a life there. They bought land for an olive grove. My grandfather replicated his clothing factories, and my grandmother went to work planting a garden, putting down new roots in this new land. They were lucky—so many of their neighbors in Syria were not.

But the violence my grandfather narrowly escaped would follow him. It would find him in the end.

I was three months old the first time I heard bombs exploding. I don't remember it, obviously, but it's a story my mom shared with me as I got older. She had taken me to Beirut, Lebanon, a beautiful city perched on the edge of the Mediterranean Sea, because her father had suffered a stroke while he was there on business. The doctors said that Jiddo Suheil was probably not going to survive and that the family should gather to say goodbye. So my mother and great-grandmother, baby in tow, took the one-hour flight from Amman to Beirut. There they reunited with my grandmother and my aunt, who lived in the city with her Lebanese husband and two young children.

In 1975, Lebanon was on the brink of a civil war, another conflict between Muslims and Christians over territory and control. For months, the city had been plagued by violent uprisings and splintering into factions, until the infamous "green line" was drawn, dividing Beirut into a Muslim West and a Christian East. But my mom didn't think much about taking me there. Often it felt as if the entire Middle East was on the brink of war. If you put your life on pause because there might be a war, your whole life would just be one big pause, and then you'd die. It's like the resting heart rate of the region is one hundred beats a minute. When that's all you know, you just get used to it.

On our second night in Beirut, the bombs began falling. My mother stayed up all night, listening to the thundering booms and rocking me on her chest, her heart pounding fast against my tiny face. All she could think about was getting us out of there.

Taytay wouldn't hear of it. We had to stay together, to stay with Jiddo Suheil, still unresponsive in the hospital. It would be safer for us to all stick together. But my mother was so scared that something might happen to me that she convinced my great-grandmother to go back to Amman with us. They got in a cab and asked the driver to head for the airport.

During war, roads to the airports get wiped out first. Talk to anyone who has had to flee a country, and they'll probably mention something about "the last plane out." The privileged ones, the ones with resources, like us, get on that plane.

But my grandmother didn't know we were safe when the radio told her that the area around the airport was destroyed in an attack. That all roads were bombed, the planes were grounded. There were no cell phones, no websites where she might check on the status of our flight. It was 1975, and it would be at least another twenty years before cell phones and websites would be invented, and another thirty before they would be commonplace. And so she thought we were dead, blown up, her mother, her daughter, her brand-new grandchild. Her husband, meanwhile, could stop breathing at any minute. She became hysterical with grief and prayed all night for a miracle.

It must have felt like one when my mother called from Amman to say that we had made it. When things subsided, my mother went back to Beirut to be with her parents, but she never took me there again. To everyone's surprise, Jiddo Suheil survived, and after many months in the hospital, he was flown back to Jordan. He was alive, but in a much different way than before. Half of his body was paralyzed, and the other weak and feeble. He could no longer form discernible words. His pale blue eyes became dark and brooding. For eleven more years, he occupied his chair in my grandparents' living room like a sentry, where sometimes he would play chess with us, motioning which piece to move with a flick of his eyes, or grunt if we put our feet on the couch. That was the grandfather I knew, not the loving, playful provider my mom remembers before that tragic day in Beirut. And while we still honored him by kissing his hand and holding it lovingly to our foreheads when we visited, my grandmother effectively took his place as the head of our family.

Sometimes I wonder if being in Beirut, the threat of war thickening the air like a dust cloud, triggered Jiddo Suheil's long-buried trauma of escaping Syria. I wonder if that's why he, by all accounts a healthy man, was seized by a stroke in the middle of the night. I know now how fear can quietly make a home in your body, like a bomb always about to explode.

TAYTAY WANTED US to remember our past, even the hard parts. Especially the hard parts. I think she saw her grandchildren living comfortably, becoming spoiled, and she worried that we didn't appreciate all that we had been given. While Jiddo Riyad and his wife gave me outrageous gifts— a piano I didn't know how to play, a red Mercedes long before I even had a license—Taytay gave us simple treats. Chocolates or pistachio-rolled ice cream: small pleasures we could enjoy together. And she went out of her way to remind us that for lots of people, even a little thing like ice cream was a big luxury.

We used to play a game before birthdays and holidays. If I had one wish, she would ask me, what would it be? I never had to think about it—I wanted a bicycle, I wanted a soccer ball, I wanted a Walkman. Then I would ask her what her wish would be. Her response was always the same.

"That everyone in the world could have clean drinking water."

"Not a new car?" I would goad her. "What about a pool?"

"I don't need those things, but people need water."

Many times I had rolled my eyes and wondered why she would waste a wish on something like that.

One afternoon when I was eight, Taytay told me to get in the car. She didn't say where we were going. At first, I was quiet, wondering where she might be taking me, but when the neighborhoods of Amman turned into the tawny hills of the countryside, my curiosity got the best of me.

"We're going to see some people," she explained.

"Which people?"

"The people at the mukhayam." Literally translated, mukhayam means "tent city." Taytay was taking me to a Palestinian refugee camp, one that had been set up decades before, when Israel was created and hundreds of thousands of Palestinians were forced to leave their homes, many with nowhere to go. The camps were supposed to be temporary, until the people there could find a new place to live, but instead they have become permanent settlements. Tent cities. At the age of eight, however, I didn't know much about that conflict or the camps. All I knew was what I heard from my dad's family—that Jordan needed to stop letting Palestinians resettle in our country. That soon they would outnumber us; they would take over everything. Why would my grandmother want me to meet the people who wanted to take over Jordan?

It only took us thirty-five minutes to get to the camp. We parked in the dirt near what looked to be the front entrance, and I hesitantly opened my door against a gust of hot desert wind. Before me, rows of tents—hundreds and hundreds of tents—fanned out toward the horizon, each modified in different, haphazard ways: extended with tarps or rugs, propped up with old umbrellas or makeshift clotheslines. In front of some there were groups of women, sitting outside on tattered mattresses sewing or visiting with each other. Trash scooted across the ground, and children tore through the narrow alleyways of canvas, maybe playing tag or maybe simply chasing one another; I couldn't tell. Everything was coated in a thick film of dust—the people included. It was chaos and filth. I had never seen anything like it, not in real life and not on TV. Fear raged in my stomach; I searched for Taytay's hands, but she was holding on to a package she had brought with her. Instead, I held fast to her skirt as we walked into the mayhem.

"Go play," she said.

"I don't want to play. I want to stay with you." Who did she want me to play with, I wondered? These poor kids running around in their dirty clothes? She had lost her mind.

Taytay knelt down beside me. "Don't ever think people are beneath you." She nodded toward a patch of land where a dozen kids were playing soccer. "Imshi," she said. *Go.*

I did as I was told. I never wanted to disappoint my grandmother.

As I approached the makeshift field, bounded by battered

tents on all sides, the children looked all the same to me. They ranged in age, but each wore the same uniform of ill-fitting hand-me-down clothes. Some of them were wearing plastic flip-flops, and others were barefoot. I suddenly felt self-conscious about my spotless polo shirt and sneakers. My anxiety eased a bit when I saw the rocks they were using as goals—my cousins and I used rocks as goals, too, when we weren't using tortoises. Maybe we had something in common after all. Everything else around me was unfamiliar and uncomfortable, but the dirt pitch and the well-loved soccer ball weren't. And like the kids on that field, the field was also my escape, the ball my security blanket.

It didn't take long for one of the kids to wave me in. At first, I ran up and down the field, following the ball, figuring out who was on my team. When I felt confident enough, I began to call for the ball by raising my arm and waving, and soon I was completely transported into the rhythm of the game. It no longer mattered that they were Palestinian and I was Jordanian, or maybe more Syrian than Jordanian. Or that they lived in a camp with thousands of people and I lived in a big house with my family. These kids were the same as me—some of them, actually most of them, were even better at soccer than I was.

We played for hours, hardly noticing the heat, the sun, our thirst. The game eventually petered out after a couple kids left and then a few more wandered off. The rest of us stood in a circle and passed around a beat-up jug of water, holding it above our lips and letting it splash into our mouths.

"I had so much fun!" I announced when I found Taytay nearby. "They were good."

Taytay's hands were now empty as we walked toward the car; she seemed distant. I wondered why she came here if it made her sad. But I knew the story of my grandparents leaving Syria, and I guessed she knew how easily it could have been our family in the mukhayam. I thought, too, about how wrong my uncles had been about Palestinians. How could they take over Jordan if they were stuck in these dirty camps? Shouldn't we welcome them? Isn't that what Allah would want us to do?

"Haram," I said to my grandmother. *Poor them.*

"Haram alayna," she corrected me, using the word's other meaning. *We are sinning.* "Don't feel sorry for them; believe in them."

We were mostly quiet on the way home from the camp, but if Taytay had asked me that day about my one wish, it sure wouldn't have been a Walkman.

CHAPTER 3
HOT DOGS AND HUMMUS

MY CHILDHOOD WAS as close to perfect as it gets. I had nothing to wish for. I was surrounded by family in a city I knew by heart. Amman was smaller back then, contained within just its seven hills, and sometimes it felt like I had memorized all of its circles and shortcuts and the flattest dirt patches to play soccer. It was a city of light and heat, of concrete and sand. It really *was* beautiful.

Amman was like two cities in one. Old and new. You could see it in the way people dressed. Older people in kamees—knee-length cotton tunics—and kaffiyehs. Young people in jeans and T-shirts or soccer jerseys; if they wore a kaffiyeh at all, it was draped around their neck.

That combination of traditional and modern found its way into our home, too. We were raised with traditional Arab family values: respect for our elders, loyalty to our family, and complete devotion to our parents. If my mother wanted something—a glass of water, a book from her nightstand—we fetched it for her. We delivered it with a kiss. The Prophet Muhammad (PBUH—*Peace Be Upon Him*; Muslims use this abbreviation to show reverence when using the name of Allah's most holy prophet) said, *Heaven is at your mother's feet,* and we made sure our mother's feet were relaxed and well rested. But our parents also brought new customs into the house, like when they declared that Friday nights were "American Night," when we ate dinners of steak and mashed potatoes, or hot dogs with macaroni and cheese. And ketchup! How I loved ketchup!

We spoke Arabic at home, but thanks to my British school and Janice—our Bajan nanny—my English, even at a very young age, was better than most Jordanian adults'. We rarely listened to Arabic music. My mother played ABBA and The Beatles. My father had collected country and Motown records while he was in college in New York; we were never allowed to touch his vinyl. I didn't notice the irony of Dolly Parton singing, *Workin' nine to five, what a way to make a livin' / Barely gettin' by, it's all takin' and no givin'* in a home we shared with a nanny, a cook, two maids, and a chauffeur. All I knew was that I loved my nanny and I really loved Dolly Parton.

Even TV was a strange combination of East and West. Every evening at five p.m., the nightly Quran reading would come on, in which a serious-looking imam would sit cross-legged in front of the holy book, reciting verses. My brothers and I would wait impatiently for it to end, and for a show we liked to start—*The Muppet Show* was our go-to, and as we got older, we loved *The Cosby Show*, *Growing Pains*, and *Are You Being Served?* These shows were all clumsily, sloppily censored for anything immoral. When characters kissed or said certain words, for instance, the screen would go black. But the censors clearly did not speak fluent English, and many phrases or situations slipped right past them. The show that got away with *everything* was *The Golden Girls*. I guess the censors figured that four old ladies couldn't be saying anything too provocative. If only they had known what was sneaking by—strong, independent women completely in charge of their lives—and how it shaped me and countless other girls in the country, maybe they would have paid more attention. Dorothy, Blanche, Rose, and Sophia were my crash course in feminism.

Our bedtime routine was very strict. At seven thirty p.m. we'd kiss our parents good night and leave them in the living room, an ashtray and a stack of magazines between them. My mother liked *Architectural Digest*, *Vogue*, and *Cosmopolitan*; my dad read *Time*, *Newsweek*, and *MAD*. We, too, would spend the next thirty minutes reading until lights out at eight p.m. Some nights my parents left after dinner to go out with friends or to a party.

My dad worked in the family business, just like all his siblings. He and four of his brothers were the vice presidents of Jiddo Riyad's three steel factories—the only three steel factories in the country at the time—and my dad managed one of the facilities. There were other "family investments" to oversee as well, including a large orange grove and several land holdings. My father's family was very much *from* Jordan, having lived in the kingdom centuries before it went by that name. My mother and her family, on the other hand, spoke endlessly of Syria, telling the same stories over and over again. When Jiddo Suheil and Taytay met my mother's Jordanian suitor, they said *no way* and *too Jordanian*. My father's accent was gruff; my mother's inflection was soft.

In their early twenties, my parents were downright progressive, my father with his shaggy hair and my mom with the Volkswagen Beetle she hand-painted with flowers. Defying Arab tradition, in which mothers largely dictate who marries whom, my parents had chosen each other after a chance meeting on the streets of Amman; soon they realized they had much in common. Both had been educated abroad (my mother in England, my father in America), both enjoyed socializing (though my mother preferred big parties and my father small gatherings). And both were Muslim, of course, but neither adhered to the more conservative tenets of the religion. They loved to travel, and during my childhood, I saw more of the world than many people get to see in their lifetime.

We went to France, England, Switzerland, and Italy. We

went to the Far East, staying in hotels in Hong Kong and Singapore where massages were free, and every day a bowl of fresh, exotic fruit appeared in the room like magic. We always traveled with extended family, and at night the adults went out for a fancy dinner while the kids indulged in room service and premium TV. We behaved ourselves. Mostly. Sometimes we'd order large meals and send them to other rooms; sometimes we banged on doors and then scurried away like bugs when a light came on.

Ali, Saeed, and I made our own fun at home, too. But we also fought like all siblings do. We wrestled, played pranks, and battled endlessly over the front seat of the Range Rover. But despite our squabbles, I loved my brothers deeply, and the three of us were fiercely devoted to one another. I helped Ali when he struggled with his schoolwork; I made sure Saeed didn't get picked on at school. For his twelfth birthday, I bought Saeed a bike. For one of Ali's, I gave him a Michael Jackson jacket and a replica of the notorious single glove. We stayed up watching videos of "Thriller," "Beat It," and "Billie Jean"; he mastered the moonwalk, and much to my father's chagrin, that jacket was glued to his body for months.

My brothers and I understood without being told that family was not just the most important thing, it was the *only* thing. This is typical in the Middle East, no matter who you are or how much money you have. For us, family members are not spokes on a bicycle wheel, they are the wheel itself. If you take out a chunk of the wheel, the wheel no longer turns; if one part of the wheel tilts left, the whole wheel rolls left. So it was for us: we were an extension of our family, not separate entities. Our middle names were our father's and our grandfather's. *Luma Hassan Riyad.* When we met someone new, their first question was "Beit meen?" *Whose house?* My answer was "Mufleh." That wasn't just my last name, it was my home. It was where and to whom I belonged.

The Middle Eastern family is so interconnected that often mothers call their children Mama, uncles call their nieces Uncle, putting into words the unity that forms the basis of everything—loyalty, love, honor.

My parents were proud Arabs. Naturally, they wanted their children to attend Arab schools. But when my kindergarten teacher swatted me with a ruler for talking out of turn, they enrolled me in an elementary school run by the British embassy. No one was allowed to hit their daughter.

The British school opened up a new world for me. Before I started there, before Janice arrived, I had never spoken English. Now I was in a classroom where instruction took place completely in English. My classmates came from all over the globe, the children of foreign diplomats. We represented many different faiths. In the mornings our headmistress, a former nun, would lead us in prayer while everyone performed the gestures that felt comfortable to them—heads bowed and hands together (for the Christians), head and hands facing the sky (for the Muslims), or eyes closed and arms folded for those who didn't know how they felt that day. At lunchtime we would gather to trade the lunches our families had packed for us. Sushi, chicken curry, egg sandwiches with mayo, and labneh sandwiches were all eagerly passed back and forth. I had my first bite of sushi in first grade, a treat from my Japanese best friend, Yuri. I learned how to say hello in six different languages. (I also learned how to curse in those same languages.)

Our teachers didn't wear hijabs. My female PE teacher wore shorts! In music class, they taught us to sing John Lennon and Bob Dylan songs and "Yellow Submarine" and "Puff the Magic Dragon." They told us to ask questions. They'd say, "What do *you* think about that?" No one had ever asked me what *I* thought about anything. At home, I had to consider how each decision I made would impact my family. At school, I got to think about me. It was satisfying and confusing at the same time. I was a quiet student, mostly, but a diligent one. I loved school. I loved to learn.

At the British school, we followed British customs. We looked forward to the enormous bonfires of Guy Fawkes Day and wore poppies on our jackets for Remembrance Day. We sang Christmas carols and put on a Christmas performance. One year I tried to get out of the family Eid celebration to be the camel in the Christmas play.

"I have to take three kings to see Jesus!" I said.

"You have to *what?*" my mother asked.

"Eissa," I said, using the Arabic word. "You know, Jesus."

"Yes, I know Jesus—"

"Well, I am the camel, and the three kings have to go see Jesus and his mother, Mary—Miriam," I explained matter-of-factly. "And it will be terrible if I don't take them."

I remember my mother's face, half-amused, half-annoyed.

"Well, *we* are celebrating Eid as a family, so the three kings will have to find another camel."

After that, my parents began to worry that maybe I was becoming a little *too* British. When I was eight, I started taking private lessons in Arabic and Islam, learning the basics of writing and reading in my mother tongue. Even though it was my native language, I had never read a book in Arabic; books in English I devoured by the dozen.

Arab in an English-speaking school. Muslim in the Christmas play. The old world of Jiddo Riyad's house and the new world of Amman. I was learning to adapt to lots of environments. To travel between worlds. To know what was okay and what wasn't in each one. Maybe that's why I felt perfectly justified to do the things that boys did—to wear pants, to be strong-willed and just plain strong.

I wanted to be like Khawlah, the infamous seventh-century Muslim warrior I learned about in my Arabic lessons, who dressed like a man to fight for Islam. Khawlah was a battlefield nurse during the Islamic conquests, but when she saw her brother taken prisoner, she threw on armor, shrouded her face, and charged the Byzantine army all by herself. I wanted to be fierce like Khawlah; I wanted to ride a horse and carry a sword. At the very least, I wanted to be prime minister of Jordan.

But my mother signed me up for ballet instead. I was horrified. A tutu and ballet slippers? Those things were not for me. I wanted to take martial arts or play soccer, but my mother insisted on ballet. I pouted, I objected, but nothing seemed to work.

During the first class, I felt so uncomfortable, like my skin was on backward.

"Please don't make me go back," I told my mother. "Let's find something else."

"This will be good for you" was her answer. "And your cousins are in the class!"

I had so many cousins that I didn't even recognize some of them. I was starting to realize that my mom used the "cousin" card to get me to do lots of things. "Your cousins are going to the party," she would say, or "Your cousins will all be there." I understood the subtext: *Don't make us look bad.*

Reluctantly, I returned to ballet. But I couldn't do the

moves. Nothing felt natural about jumping or standing on my tiptoes in tight shoes. My body, or maybe my brain, wouldn't let me. After a while, I gave up and sat down in frustration.

The teacher asked me to stand. I didn't want to be disrespectful to the teacher, so I said nothing and sat still. She asked me to stand again. I was silent. She told me to leave the class.

I hurried out to find my mom waiting for me in the parking lot and felt a mixture of relief and panic, a sickness in my stomach for being so rude to the teacher.

That night at home, my mother was disappointed. "It's important for you to play sports," she lectured. What she meant was that it was important I play *girls'* sports, not the ones I liked, the ones that were considered more masculine— soccer, cricket, tennis. My mother herself had been an athlete, excelling in track and basketball when she was young, two sports that were acceptable for a young lady in Arab culture.

"Ballet is not a sport."

"Mama, it *is* a sport," she insisted.

"Is there anything else I can play? I will try anything."

"There's a new team that the Americans are starting up," my father interjected over the newspaper. He meant the American school at the American embassy. "Little League baseball."

"What is baseball?" I had never heard that word.

"It's like rounders, or cricket, with a ball and a bat—but American."

I loved rounders and cricket; this could work, I thought. My dad signed my brothers and me up.

Coach Cooper had an accent like the police officers on *CHiPs*. He had white hair and tucked his T-shirt into his jeans. The first time he threw a ball to me, I instinctively tossed my glove off so I could catch it with my hands. He gently explained that the more I used the glove, the softer it would be. The more it would move with my hand. He taught me how to hold a bat and throw a ball, how to make my glove softer by wrapping it around a ball and laying it under my mattress. A former marine who now worked for the US embassy in Jordan, he was tough, gentle, and kind.

I began with T-ball and moved up to coach-pitch and finally kid-pitch. Because the league required that two girls be on the field at all times, I got to play a lot. At home, I practiced by throwing the ball against the wall. Ali, Saeed, and I played catch any chance we got.

Fridays were game days, the highlight of my week. I loved watching my brothers' games, and they always cheered during mine. Because of the neighborhood's heightened security, the field was enclosed by a towering stone wall. It made the space feel secret and safe. We would sit on the wall, watching the day's games go by, the dirt and dust flying in every direction. Our parents rarely stayed to watch but always gave us a little money so that we could buy lunch. I would tuck it in my shoes (baseball pants didn't have pockets), and when we couldn't resist the temptation any longer, we would run to the concession stand, ready to double up on our American food intake. We'd down chili dogs and hamburgers and our weekly allowance of soda. Dr Pepper for me, Mirinda for Ali, and 7UP for Saeed.

Everything that felt wrong about ballet—wearing a tight pink outfit and performing alone—was missing from baseball. I found out that I felt the happiest playing with a ball, whether it was a baseball or basketball or soccer ball. On the field or on the court, I felt relaxed and at ease physically, but also emotionally. I liked knowing that I was a part of a team and that my teammates were my friends; they had my back. We would laugh and celebrate together or get frustrated and grumble together. Either way, we were together with one uniting purpose—to score and to win. And for a brief moment in time, nothing else mattered except for that.

CHAPTER 4
NO WORD FOR WHAT I AM

MY FIRST CRUSH was a girl named Isabella. She was the daughter of diplomats, half British and half Malay, with shiny brown hair and bangs that framed her freckled face. During fifth grade, she would come over to my house, and we would swim and climb trees and dream about starting our own secret society, kind of like the Famous Five, so we could solve mysteries and have adventures. Isabella was by far the prettiest girl in school, and maybe the nicest, too. She resisted all the cliques that everyone else had arranged themselves into and was kind to everyone—including me. She thought I was a good soccer player, and she liked the poem I wrote in English class about an ostrich. Isabella inflated my ego, and part of me thought she might have a crush on me, too.

My friends Justin and Michael also had crushes on Isabella. Michael was a better soccer player than me, and Justin got better grades in math, but all around I thought I had the best chance. One day, Justin, Michael, and I were on the playground, and the topic of Isabella came up.

"I think she likes me," said Michael.

"No she doesn't," I responded.

"How do you know?" Justin asked.

"I just do."

"Well, why don't you ask her if she likes me or Justin?" Michael asked.

"Yeah, go and ask her," Justin echoed.

Normally, I would have thrown my hat in the ring. But something made me hesitate. Something about this moment felt different. A certain knowledge seemed to come into focus then, the result of countless subtle messages that all said the same thing. Only boys liked girls.

Isabella ran over when she saw me walking toward her. I felt my heart do the little flip it did when Isabella looked at me. It was a feeling I both enjoyed and despised.

"You're not playing soccer today?" she asked.

"No, it's too hot, and everyone else is playing hopscotch or dodgeball."

"Yeah, it's so hot," she said.

"Anyway, they"—I pointed behind me to Justin and Michael—"want to know. Well, they want to know—"

"If I like Justin or Michael?" she completed my thought.

Or me? I wanted to say. But like Justin and Michael, she didn't even see me as a part of the equation.

"I think I like Michael. What do you think?"

"He's a good soccer player, but he doesn't get good grades," I said.

"Well then, Justin."

"But he can't even kick a ball."

"That's true." Isabella spun her hair around a finger, contemplating.

"There is no one else?" I asked, trying to hide the twinge of hope in my voice.

"No, I think it's Michael. He's cuter."

And that was that; she had made her decision, and it was not me.

I knew Isabella didn't think to choose me because I was a girl. All during elementary school, I had hung out with boys. I listened to them talk about their crushes—about which girls were pretty and which girls were funny—and I'd jump in, agreeing or disagreeing with their assessments. But now that we were almost in middle school, things were different. I began to realize that *I* was different.

The feeling I had in ballet—that my skin was on backward—I started feeling it all the time. Like what people saw on the outside was not who I was on the inside. Like I had been given a dark secret to hold on to, and if people knew, they would hate me. I wouldn't get picked for teams, invited to parties. I'd probably not even be cast as a camel in the school play.

· · ·

THE FEELING PERSISTED as I began middle school. The Amman Baccalaureate School was selective and expensive— the who's who of Jordan's most prominent families. If it had been up to me, I would have stayed with my friends at the British school for sixth grade, but my parents were increasingly concerned about my weakness in written Arabic, about the fact that I had no Arab friends. At the Baccalaureate School, instruction would be in Arabic and English, and I would also have to take classes on Islam, another subject I needed extra help in. Virtually all of the students there were Arab.

Gone were the days of "Puff the Magic Dragon" and trading labneh sandwiches for chicken curry. The kids at my new school were merciless. If you were different in any way—if you didn't wear a ponytail or spend your weekends at the city's posh athletic club—you were an outcast. They made fun of the Syrian accent I had inherited from my mother. They made fun of me for hanging out with the boys. They made fun of the way that I dressed. The bullying was relentless. I longed to go back to Yuri, Michael, Justin, and Isabella.

At the Baccalaureate School, girls could either wear pants or skirts. I always wore pants. I liked to play soccer during recess, and pants were better for that. All the other girls wore skirts. I didn't even really notice until one of them said, "I like your pants." It took me a second to realize she was mocking me.

I reluctantly started wearing a skirt—but I wore shorts underneath it so I could still play soccer at recess.

One day, not long after I started wearing a skirt, a group of boys kept turning around in class, looking at me and then dissolving into laughter. I was confused. I ran my hands over my face to see if something was on it. Finally, the girl sitting next to me leaned in and said, "Close your legs."

I snapped my knees together, but Osama was laughing. "I saw your underwear!" he said.

"You couldn't have seen my underwear, because I have shorts on!" I yelled back.

I immediately regretted saying it.

The laughter grew louder, and everyone was exchanging funny looks.

"Why would you have shorts under your skirt?"

I shrank in my seat and smiled like I was in on the joke.

From then on, it became my mission to be invisible, to blend in as much as possible. But that proved hard to do.

A few days later, in history class, we were learning about the Jordanian monarchy. The teacher explained that the current ruler, King Hussein, was only seventeen when he took the throne, so it was a small group of advisors who had mostly run the country during the early years of his reign. Even now that Hussein was well into his forties, many of those advisors continued to be powerful influences, the teacher said. He listed those men's names, starting with Riyad Mufleh. My face burned as all eyes turned to me.

I always knew my family was influential, I just hadn't known *how* influential. When I was young, we got away with things others wouldn't have, like when my cousin Omar and I took the keys to Taytay's car and crashed it into a tree down the block. If we had been normal kids, our fathers would have been thrown in jail. But because we were Muflehs, the police ended up apologizing to us instead.

Invisible, it seemed, wasn't an option.

Jumana's father was Palestinian; her mother, American. A constellation of freckles stretched out across her perfect olive skin, and her wavy brown hair cascaded halfway down her back.

Jumana was the most pretty *and* popular seventh grader at the Baccalaureate School, so I kept my distance. But sometimes, watching her walk across the cafeteria or talking to her friends at recess, my heart would spin around in that same way it had with Isabella.

"My mom knows your mom," Jumana said the first time we talked. I had been throwing a ball against the wall after lunch with Adam, who, at the beginning of seventh grade, was basically my only friend. With his dark red hair and British accent, Adam was a clear outsider. We had that in common. That day, the day Jumana approached us on the playground, Adam and I had just been minding our own business, working on our pitch.

"So?" I said, feeling awkward and unsure.

"So she said I should be friends with you because you don't have any."

"I don't need any friends."

"Come on, let's just take a walk," she insisted.

And then it happened. Jumana smiled at me. It felt like all the blood in my veins had been replaced with electricity.

I glanced at Adam, hoping I'd see an expression of approval on his face, but he was looking down, concentrating on being invisible.

I went with Jumana. She led me around the playground and over to her group of friends, every one of them with a perky ponytail and perfectly pleated skirt. Whatever confidence I felt being next to Jumana disintegrated as they all turned to look at me.

"I like your pants," a girl from my history class said.

"My pants?" I repeated, sure the girl was making fun of me, just like Osama had.

"Yeah, they're cool."

"They're uniform pants, same as everyone else's," I said, shrugging.

At this, Jumana flipped her body away from the group, with her mouth close to my ear.

"Quit being so rude."

"Rude?"

"Yes, she's just trying to talk to you. It's hard to talk to you, you know."

"It's not hard to talk to me," I said, turning my head so that I could see Jumana's face.

"Yes, it is. You think you're smarter than everyone else."

"Maybe I just don't like being around stupid people."

It was strange. I didn't *want* to be mean to Jumana. I didn't *want* to walk away. But I did both of those things because I wasn't sure what else to do.

Luckily, Jumana didn't give up on me. Every time we'd pass in the hallway, she'd give me one of those irresistible smiles. I couldn't help but smile back. Sometimes I'd go out to eat with my family and see her with hers. One day, Jumana invited me over to her house. I wondered if her mom had made her ask me, but I didn't care enough not to go. That afternoon we lay on her bedroom floor, flipping through teen magazines, which had finally made their way to Jordan.

Like all middle school friendships, ours was immediate and intense. The next day, she asked me to come over again. And then again after that. Soon, I hardly saw Adam, I was so inseparable from Jumana. She was pretty much the only thing I could think about. Sometimes, when I went over to her house, I would play basketball with her brother, something that made her jealous (which made me feel good). Sometimes, I talked about a book she hadn't read, which made her pretend to be annoyed with me (which also made me feel good). All of a sudden, I was one of the popular people; I was invited to the birthdays and pool parties and even hosted one myself.

We were watching a movie when Jumana slipped her hand into mine.

I pulled it away.

She pulled it right back. "You're my best friend. You're the only one I can be myself around."

I rolled my eyes but didn't let go of her hand. "Watch the movie."

"You're so mean," Jumana said, but didn't let go of my hand either.

What did this mean? I held hands with my aunt Abla, my cousin Lana, and other female relatives all the time; in Jordan, it wasn't uncommon for male friends to hold hands. But with Jumana, it felt different. It *was* different, I hoped.

A few weeks later, when I left with my family for our summer vacation in Cyprus, Jumana and I had held hands so many times. Each time her knuckles slid between my fingers, I felt the same blood-quickening rush. I started to think that Jumana liked me the way I liked her. I let myself believe that I wasn't a freak after all.

I thought about Jumana every day while I was gone. While I was waterskiing in the Mediterranean or enduring long dinners with my parents or playing childish pranks on my cousins. As soon as we got back to Amman, I called Jumana.

"Can you hang out today?" I asked, rubbing my thumb against one of the seashells I had collected for her from the beach.

"I can't, I have friends over." Jumana's voice sounded different. It sounded hard and far away.

"Okay, well, how about tomorrow? I have so many stories to tell you."

"I can't. I'm going over to Fahed's house tomorrow."

Fahed? I wondered. He was in our circle of friends, a nice boy with a big pool. He had invited us all over a few times and even come over to my house, too.

"Why?" I asked. "Is he having a pool party?"

"No, we're hanging out and watching a movie. He's my boyfriend."

So I was a friend who happened to be a girl, but not a girlfriend. My relationship with Jumana ended as immediately and intensely as it started.

I hung up and crushed the seashells I had gotten her from the beach. The next week at school, I found Adam at our usual spot.

. . .

THE EXTRA ATTENTION I got for being Riyad Mufleh's grand-daughter didn't last too long. After all, the Baccalaureate School was full of rich and powerful offspring, including the king's own children.

Talal was the one in my grade. He was plain-looking and short, with dark hair and dark eyes. Every morning, he was delivered to school by a caravan of black cars, his security detail. Until middle school, he had been educated in England. His Arabic had a British cadence to it that seemed to embarrass him; he tried to cover it up with an over-the-top Arabic inflection. Sometimes he'd talk about his famous parents in a way that made them seem compli-cated and normal.

To me, there wasn't much that was notable about Talal; he was just another boy I played soccer with at recess. (And if I'm honest, he wasn't very good. There are some things money can't buy, and athletic ability is one of them.) But all the other girls were crazy about Talal. They wanted to date a prince. I think Talal chose me to like—even though my ponytail was wild and I wore shorts under my skirt—because I was the only girl who didn't fawn over him. It was my cousin who told me Talal had a crush on me, then some girls from my class said the same. I decided to avoid him until the whole thing blew over.

It was a school night, a couple months after Jumana and I last held hands, when Talal's three cars pulled up outside my house unannounced. I thought for sure my parents would turn him away; we weren't allowed to have friends over on weeknights, especially if they didn't call ahead to get permission. But I found out rules don't apply to royalty.

They let him in and left us in the sitting room together. While we sat and talked about school and sports, I felt annoyed by his presumption. I had homework to do. I counted down the minutes until it was time for him to leave.

Talal kept coming back. On one of his visits he brought a framed photograph of himself, signed at the bottom with the inelegant signature of a preteen. He told me to put it by my bed. If he had been any other boy, my parents would have put an end to this courtship firmly and immediately— dating wasn't really a thing that thirteen-year-olds did in Arab culture. Instead, they instructed me to just be nice to him. But soon, by our classmates' definition, we were officially "dating," whatever that means in an Arab middle school.

All of a sudden, my star was on the rise once again. The girls at school cornered me, asking questions about what Talal was like in private, what we talked about when we were together. I didn't know what to tell them. I certainly couldn't tell them that the feeling between Talal and me was not mutual. That I didn't like him; that, really, it was his sister I was infatuated with. She rode horses and didn't try to hide her sophisticated British accent. It made me feel defective, like there was something very wrong with me. What would these girls think about me if they knew the truth?

I stuck it out for forty-three long days (I kept count). On the forty-fourth day, Talal had a birthday party at the palace. It was December, and the whole place was decked out in Christmas decorations. I tried my best to dodge him, but somehow Talal and I ended up alone. I panicked when I realized this; girls were never supposed to be alone with boys. Ever. Where were my friends? How did this happen?

"Do you know what that is?" he asked, pointing to a cluster of dangling mistletoe. I forced a smile hoping he would drop it. Wishing it were his sister standing beneath this garland with me. "Do you know what we're supposed to do under it?" His face was now looming close to mine.

I didn't think about slapping Talal, I just did it. It was instinct. He looked shocked, but I didn't feel sorry. He marched out of the room, his footsteps echoing on the marble floor, and I breathed a deep sigh of relief. That night, when I put Talal's photo in the trash, it hit me: if a real-life prince couldn't sway me, there was no hope that I would ever like a boy.

Talal told everyone at school that he was the one who broke it off. That was fine with me. He could keep his secret, and I would keep mine.

. . .

THERE ISN'T A word that means "gay" in Arabic. There were no gay characters on TV, and not in books either. Romeo loved Juliet, Pip loved Estella, Clark Kent loved Lois Lane. It was the 1980s; there was no internet, no Google. How those things would have changed my life. Given me some way to know what I was and that I wasn't alone.

Instead, I was like a stone stuck in the middle of a rushing current. All the girls who were once tomboys (the ones good at sports) were growing out of that phase. Boys who were once shy and awkward were asking girls to school dances. This was just the natural way of things: boys like girls, and girls like boys. They grow up and get married and have kids. Life seemed so easy for everyone else.

My life, meanwhile, seemed to be getting progressively harder from one year to the next so that when I thought of getting older, of going to college or university, I would feel paralyzed by fear. I could barely handle middle school! When I thought about the future, I would get stuck. I could visualize little things, like moving on to the next grade, winning soccer tournaments, or family cookouts. But there was so much I couldn't see. I couldn't see friends that I could truly be myself with, I couldn't see dancing with someone at a school dance, and I certainly couldn't see a wedding, which some of the girls already liked to fantasize about.

I found myself daydreaming about being back on the playground with Justin and looking for bugs or exchanging food with Yuri as we solved our math problems. I remembered longingly the big family dinners of my childhood, when I would run and play all afternoon and evening with my favorite cousins, Omar and Lana. I was beginning to think that the only place I truly fit in was the past.

Once, my grandmother had explained that our religion doesn't permit tattoos, because we believe it is wrong to alter the body that Allah has created. *He creates each one of us exactly how we are for a reason,* she said. But I struggled to understand what reason Allah had in mind when he created me.

It felt so unfair. I was praying five times almost every day. Sometimes I prayed extra so that Allah might change me. I fasted; I was kind and compassionate; I was a good student and an obedient daughter. But nothing happened. I was still me, and there still was no word for that.

CHAPTER 5
KHAROOF

THE PRESSURE TO be more feminine at home started well before middle school. My mother had urged me to wear skirts and dresses and behave in a more ladylike way for as long as I could remember. On vacation, she would take me shopping and dress me up like a doll. We weren't allowed to wear makeup to school, but she encouraged me to put it on if we were going to a party or family get-together. For bigger events, she hired someone to come do her makeup, and sometimes I would let them do mine, too, hoping it would get me off the hook for a while.

"They're so beautiful!" the makeup artist said about my eyes. "She doesn't need anything on them."

"But imagine how much *more* beautiful they could be with a little something," my mother responded. Whether it was her house or garden or daughter, my mother always wanted everything to be *more* beautiful.

She was the kind of woman who never left home without makeup. Her hair was almost always impeccably coiffed, her closet full of Valentino and Chanel, silk and satin. My mother expected that I would like all those things, too—the mall, getting my hair done—but I didn't. I hated those things. I desperately wanted to please her, but I felt ridiculous in the outfits she picked out; the makeup made me feel like an alien.

It wasn't like my mother was an anomaly. Almost all of the older women I knew growing up were obsessed with their appearance. My mom, for all of her fussiness, was nowhere near as fancy as some of her friends. But like many Arabs, my parents put a lot of stock into what other people thought of them and their children. Something as simple as riding my bike in a pair of shorts could earn me a lecture. My aversion to feminine activities and my insistence on traditionally masculine ones, like playing soccer, were disappointing to my mother, who had also once been a great athlete—before she grew up to be a glamorous woman. I felt like she was waiting for me to grow out of who I was. Or maybe I felt like that because *I* was waiting to grow out of who I was. Waiting to grow into the person who was more like everyone else.

If it was going to happen, I figured it would happen soon. I knew that girls changed around middle school, that they became women. I hoped that becoming a woman meant I would like all the things I was supposed to like—including boys.

My first period was a terrifying, traumatic experience. No one had warned me. I thought I had been gravely injured by a fight I had broken up between my cousins the week before. I went home early from school, after the nurse assured me what was happening was normal.

"This is not normal," I insisted. "Bleeding is not normal, and bleeding from down there is definitely not normal."

"Why don't we call your mom?" she said as she pulled a pad out of her desk drawer and instructed me to put it in my underwear.

Now I wasn't just bleeding from between my legs, I was wearing a diaper, too.

My mother and Taytay were both waiting for me at home, beaming like a movie star had just walked into the living room.

"You're a woman now!" my mother said, curling me up in her arms.

"Mama, I am injured. I might be dying. Why are you smiling?"

Taytay laughed and pulled me onto her lap. "Your mom should have told you this sooner, but when girls are a certain age, they get their cycle. They bleed once a month. This means you are a woman now."

"Once a month? For a whole day?"

Now both women laughed. "Three days," Taytay said. "Maybe four or five."

Bleeding every month from between my legs? That's what made me a woman? The pain in my stomach was nothing compared to the storm raging in my head. I was a woman. But nothing had changed. I still liked girls. Whatever it was that was defective about me—was it permanent?

There were more changes to come. I had to start wearing a bra. My mom bought me some frilly, flowery things I shoved to the back of the drawer. I felt much more comfortable in a sports bra.

The hair on my arms grew in thick and dark. My aunt Abla, my favorite aunt and my mother's favorite sister, teased me by affectionately calling me kharoof—*sheep* (which I much preferred over gorilla, the word my middle-school bullies used). The ridicule from my classmates about my clothes and my body hair and the pressure from my family to be feminine was enough to make me actually consider wearing a hijab so no one could see me. Maybe then everyone would just leave me alone. If only it were that simple.

It was a weekend morning when Aunt Abla and my mother called me into my parents' bathroom. When I arrived in the doorway, three women smiled back at me: my aunt, my mom, and a very short older woman I had seen before. Her name was Nuzha. She had surgical gloves on and was massaging a gooey ball of something in her hands. I knew what was happening.

"I don't want it!" I yelped.

"You're going to love it," my mother said, putting her arm around my shoulders and leading me into the room.

"You're going to look so much prettier," Abla said. She pulled the hem of my top up toward my face as I instinctually lifted my arms.

When my brothers and I were young, the doctor used to come to our house to give us our vaccines. We hated the shots, so we would run outside and hide in the olive trees. That's exactly what I wanted to do now.

Instead, I was stark naked, sitting in a kitchen chair that had been placed in the middle of the floor. The countertops around me were a nauseous swirl of pink and orange, giving the whole room a rosy cast. The air was still and heavy with the smell of my mom's perfume.

My mother stood close, and Abla sat on the edge of the tub. They kept their hands on their knees, ready in case I made a break for it.

Nuzha took my hand. She grinned as she smoothed the warm goo over my forearm. I remembered overhearing my mom and aunt talking about how good this woman was at what she did. She was the best, they said. I watched her every move, determined to be brave.

"Deep breath," Nuzha said.

I heard it before I felt it, a loud ripping sound. My skin burned, tingled, and then went numb.

I couldn't help it: I screamed.

"Oh, stop being a baby," Nuzha snapped. "That wouldn't hurt anyone."

Abla squeezed my knee and laughed. "It hurts, right?"

"I wax girls younger than you—and they just sit there," Nuzha said, massaging the wax into the next strip of hair.

"Sit there? What are they, dead?"

She yanked again.

"Yilan abouki!" I yelled. *I curse your father.* I looked over at my mom to see if I was in trouble, but she just laughed.

"Yilan imek," Nuzha cursed my mother with another, faster yank.

(Never curse at a woman who is waxing you.)

"Look at this." She held the wax out so I could see all of the hair embedded in it.

"I told you—kharoof." Aunt Abla laughed. "This will be the most hair you ever remove."

Nuzha went back to work. I set my jaw and watched as she repeated the process over and over again, on my arms and legs, and everywhere else. First the warmth, then the snap, then the dull numbness.

After about an hour, Nuzha was done.

"Feel yourself!" Abla said.

I ran my hands over my arms and legs. I couldn't help but smile. I had survived. And I was soft.

"See? You've got skin under there." My mother smiled. She and my aunt seemed proud of me. I was proud of myself. Finally, a rite of passage I didn't fail miserably. Now when I wore a skirt to school or changed for gym class, I wouldn't have to feel self-conscious.

I couldn't change my accent. I couldn't help who I had a crush on. But I could hold my breath, take the pain, and curse at Nuzha. It gave me a little bit of hope.

CHAPTER 6
THE THRESHOLD

MY AUNT ABLA was the only one of my mother's siblings who was born in Jordan, having made the drive from Damascus curled up safely in my grandmother's belly. She was the baby of the family, much beloved, inheriting both the family's blond hair and blue eyes and its playful nature. Because she was only ten years older than me, Abla seemed different from all my other aunts, almost like a best friend or a sister. She was fun and funny, magic and magnetic—and impossibly cool.

When my parents went out of town (and they went out of town a lot), Abla would come over to stay with us. During these weeks, our home—normally a sanctuary of routine and decorum—would transform into a playground of open doors and midnight snacks. Abla slept in my parents' bedroom, a space I typically only saw in the yellow light before school, when Ali, Saeed, and I would tiptoe in to kiss their sleeping cheeks goodbye. With Abla in it, the room was wholly different. Everything that was usually not allowed in the room was not only permitted but highly encouraged. We watched TV and ate bags of potato chips and chocolates on the bed. We'd stay up late watching shows we'd only heard our parents talk about. We'd stay up *so* late we'd hear the national anthem that came on every night at the end of the day's programming. And we didn't even stand up when it played!

All the while, Abla would be on the phone with her friends, complaining about teachers, gossiping about boys, and planning their next outing. I'd split my attention down the middle—between forbidden TV shows and the fascinating contents of these conversations. Abla seemed to tell her friends everything, things she would never tell her mother or even mine. I wondered if I would ever have a group of friends like this; I wondered if I'd ever be able to tell someone all of my secrets.

Lots of rules just didn't seem to apply to my favorite aunt. Or she just figured out ways to get around them. When she found out my mom wouldn't let me cut my hair short (which I badly wanted), Abla massaged gum into it, forcing my mother's hand. She hated fancy clothes and makeup and dressed as she pleased in jeans and T-shirts (still managing to outshine every woman in the room). Like my mother, Abla didn't wear a hijab. She was also openly critical of the superconservative strains of Islam that required women to shroud their entire bodies. Many women in Jordan viewed the burka as an import from more oppressive societies like Iran and Saudi Arabia; it had no place in a modern country like ours. Multiple times I watched in awe as Abla confronted women in full burkas, asking, *Who is in there? Aren't you hot? How can you see?*

When I was twelve, Abla was finishing up college, the first female in my mother's family to do so. She had made lots of friends at university and, even though she was twenty-two, still had to ask permission to hang out with them. Taytay was always hesitant; young women were not supposed to go out on their own. Traditionally, a mother would have sent an older male to chaperone, but Taytay always sent me. Surely, she must have thought, Abla would not do anything bad in front of her impressionable young niece.

I treasured the time it was just Abla and me in the car. Sometimes we stopped for ice cream or drove around looking for our favorite street vendors to buy whatever fruit was in season. Abla usually haggled, usually got something for free, and always gave the vendors a huge tip. Sometimes, she would bring along a gorilla mask she got from who knows where. When we would stop at a traffic light, she would put it on and look over at the driver of the car next to us. First they would jump, then they would laugh, all while I tried—and failed—to keep a straight face.

During the spring of her senior year, Abla began regularly taking me to Tom & Jerry, an American restaurant in a neighborhood called Shmeisani, about ten minutes from our house. I was doubly delighted about these outings: hanging out with Abla anywhere was a thrill in itself—plus, Tom & Jerry had *the* best chocolate milkshakes, a heavenly treat I hadn't known existed until then.

This was before McDonald's or any other fast-food chain had made it to Jordan. Even though Amman was an enormous capital, it often felt like a small village. The arrival of a Western establishment could create a kind of singular excitement; it seemed everyone in the city had tried—and loved—Tom & Jerry. There was something so new and exciting about ordering at the counter and carrying your tray to any table you wanted, something enticing about the way they wrapped the food in colorful striped and checked paper. That sounds silly now, but the laid-back, have-it-your-way air of a fast-food restaurant felt kinetic. It felt like a party. Tom & Jerry was the first place where I had a fountain drink. For Abla, though, our trips to Tom & Jerry were not about the sodas or even the milkshakes. They were about seeing Kareem.

After we paid for our food, Abla would walk me to a table in the corner of the restaurant, where I was to sit and read while she socialized. But I would only pretend to read, peering over my book instead to watch as Abla took her place at the long table full of her friends—always in the same spot, always in the seat across from Kareem. Most Arab men have beards, or at least a mustache, but Kareem did not, and so there was no hiding his lips or his teeth or just how happy he was to see Abla. My aunt seemed to float in her chair in front of him, buoyant in his presence. While the others would banter and carry on, Abla and Kareem spoke only to each other, as if they were the only two people at this party—surrounded by a rainbow of discarded wrapping paper and the potent smell of junk food.

Kareem appeared mild-mannered and good-hearted, but for Abla, Kareem was pure rebellion. Not only was she keeping secrets from Taytay, she was seeing a man from a different, lower class. It was thrilling to watch her bust through the biggest, most taboo barrier yet.

On the way home from these outings, too many of us crammed into Abla's tiny Renault, her friends would ask if I thought Kareem was handsome while Abla grinned at me in the rearview mirror.

"Yeah, sure," I said, trying not to let on how exciting it felt to be asked. I was the twelve-year-old hanging out with the cool kids; the twenty-two-year-olds wanted my opinion. Obviously, this guy wasn't my type (in any sense of the word, but no one needed to know that), but this question wasn't just a question—it was an invitation, entry to a world I hadn't known existed, a place where we could be ourselves. It was as if Abla was telling me, *The adults and their rules are crazy; we are different.* Watching Abla sit across from her secret crush filled me with hope. That there were other people like me, who wanted things we weren't supposed to want. That it was *okay* to want those things. That maybe one day I could share an hour and a milkshake with a girl I liked while one of my nieces (perhaps Abla's daughter!) ran cover. Abla never told me not to tell; she just knew that I wouldn't. Our trust, like our bond, went unspoken.

IN THE MONTHS leading up to Abla's college graduation, while we had been at Tom & Jerry, my grandmother had been entertaining a parade of young men and their mothers in the living room of her home. These visits were more like job interviews, and the job was to be Abla's husband. It was a given that soon after she finished school, Abla would marry and start a family of her own.

People think that arranged marriages are loveless, but that's not true. They're all about love, actually, familial love. But when you marry, you don't just marry the person, you marry their family, and they marry yours. Who you marry ultimately becomes part of your extended family, and they have to fit neatly into it. This is why, during the matchmaking process, every member voices their opinion: your brother, your aunt, your third cousin twice removed. This way, all the members of the family are invested in the success of the marriage.

If the Middle Eastern family is a bicycle wheel, then marriage means adding another wheel to the bike. If the wheels are a bad match—if they're shaped differently or one is wobbly—the bike, marriage, won't get very far. The families don't prosper.

In Arab culture, matchmaking is handled by the women. When it's time for their daughters and sons to wed, Arab mothers go on the hunt for the right partner. They start off by assembling an FBI-caliber file on every potential match. They ask neighbors and friends and grocery store clerks what they know about the potential match and their family. Do they drink? If so, is it beer or whiskey? (Both are bad, but liquor is worse.) Do they gamble? (A deal breaker.) Do they have a temper? (Not a deal breaker, but a red flag.) Most importantly, how do they treat their sisters and female relatives? Our mothers are calculating and cunning, experts in interrogation, in getting anyone to confess family secrets over an innocent cup of tea. Dating app algorithms have nothing on *mamas*. They're excellent at what they do.

So much so that most children trust their mothers with this task. To find someone who will complement and care for them. And most of the time, the choice is not mandated. The matchmaking process typically ends not in a daughter being forced into marriage, but in her approval—and her peace of mind that her marriage will be supported by both families.

Still, when Abla agreed to marry Yousef, I was stunned. Out of the many men she could have chosen, I didn't understand why it was him. Yousef was seven years older than Abla, the dark hair around his crown beginning to thin. Unlike Kareem, Yousef wore a thick mustache that concealed his mouth and his moods. There was nothing special about him.

"We will call him Joseph!" Abla joked with me, as if giving him a Western name might make up for his Middle Eastern plainness.

But this time, Abla's playfulness was no match for the truth. I was losing her. Yousef was taking her away—from our family to his family, from our house to his. This wasn't just a youthful crush like Kareem. Soon she would have children of her own and no more time for me.

In the weeks after the decision was made, Abla campaigned for me to like Yousef. She took me to the movies with them, and even to get fast food. But Yousef was damned from the beginning. No one was good enough for Abla. (Well, maybe some mix of Michael J. Fox and David Bowie, but that was beginning to look increasingly unlikely.) More painful still, with Yousef there, these outings no longer felt special. I was no longer a part of Abla's secret world, *our* secret world.

She would marry him and live by the rules I'd thought did not apply to us. One day, I would have to do the same.

YOUSEF AND ABLA had their first child, Sara, around the same time that my mother had my sister, Inam. I had begged my parents for a sister for much of my childhood, and their response was always the same: "Maybe if you pray to Allah, he will give you a sister." When my mother told me she was pregnant, I felt an enormous sense of accomplishment. I had done it—I had prayed my baby sister into existence.

Of course, soon in biology class I learned how my mother had really become pregnant. I was furious. Why had they lied? Why had they pretended that having babies was up to Allah when it had been their choice the whole time?

I began to see it everywhere, the way adults used Allah to get their way. Inshallah, they always said, *if Allah wills it*. Allah, I had been told, had ninety-nine names: the Just, the Gentle, the Ever-Forgiving, the Most Merciful, to name a few. And yet Allah did not will so many things that he should have. When my dad's mother was diagnosed with lung cancer, I was told to pray so that Allah would make her healthy. When that didn't work, I was told to pray for her not to suffer. But all I remember about her now is that Allah let her face turn stiff and white as chalk. Why hadn't Allah stopped the violence in Syria so that Taytay could watch her flower beds bloom each spring? Why didn't the Palestinian children I had played soccer with in the mukhayam have a home and a school?

If I were Allah, my dad's mom would not have died of cancer and her family would not have suffered watching her turn into a shell of what she was. If I were Allah, every kid would have food, a bed and a home, and a soccer ball. If I were Allah, Syria's brutal dictator, Hafez al-Assad—not my grandfather—would have been the one paralyzed, in a wheelchair, not being able to feed himself.

Once I saw it, I couldn't stop seeing it. On the way to one of my baseball practices, our driver, Abed, offered a ride home to Rahmeh, our amazing cook. When we arrived at her home, in a part of Amman I had never been to, I was mortified to see her run-down house, hardly much bigger than our kitchen. Watching her children and grandchildren emerge happily to greet her was the first time I considered that after a long day of filling our bellies with delicious food, this woman returned to feed her own hungry family, who clearly made do with much less than ours. I learned that Janice, who wore a pink apron and smelled like cocoa butter, had left a young son when she emigrated from Barbados to take care of someone else's children so that hers could have a better life. Janice loved us like we were her own. Why hadn't Allah willed our cook a bigger home and a never-ending buffet of food or Janice a life not separated from her son?

I began spending more and more time alone. I retreated to the roof of our home, where I could listen to music and be close to the clouds; I liked to watch them dance across the sky on their way to somewhere else. But soon even my quiet refuge was invaded by loud cries of protest. The Jordanian government, deeply in debt, had raised the price of bread, and Amman had erupted into riots. I stared as, just beyond the high walls and metal gates of our property, the protesters vandalized and looted the neighborhood. What they were doing didn't seem right, but I felt guilty: I could buy a stack of warm pita bread with just the change I found in my pockets. Why did our family have so much, and others so little? I thought of my grandmother's words: *haram alayna.*

There were so many feelings that I didn't know what to do with. So I pushed them down. Down past my chest, down past my stomach. I pushed them down into my legs and into my feet, where they turned into fire and thrust me around baseball diamonds, around tennis courts, around soccer fields. I pushed them down; I ran and ran and ran.

WHEN I WAS a kid, I loved weddings. If there's one thing Arabs know how to do, it's weddings. Every one of them is like a Kardashian wedding. The bride decked out from head to toe in her new family's jewels. The six-foot-tall wedding cakes carved by a gold-plated sword. Women in sparkly dresses, men in fezzes, and platters upon platters of food. So many flowers, you'd forget we lived in the desert. I'd never want the night to end, as my little cousins fell asleep one by one beneath the tables, only to be woken up by the fireworks display—yes, always fireworks—for the happy couple.

My favorite part was the dancing. I didn't like dancing much, but wedding dances were the exception because they weren't just about boys dancing with girls; they were communal. I loved watching the zaffeh, when a band of Syrian drummers pound the tabla so hard the room would shake as the bride and groom walked into the reception hall. The performers, dressed in traditional clothing (black MC Hammer pants, a white shirt with big sleeves, a vest, and a fez), would get everyone to clap along with excitement and then perform the sword-fight dance, leaping and twirling around the room while clashing the swords against each other to the beat of the drum. My other favorite dance was the dabke, or line dance, when everyone got in on the action, holding hands and kicking their legs.

It is too much of everything: food, music, dancing, flowers, and cotton candy. It is the most joy and extravagance that you will ever see in one room.

It seemed someone in our enormous family was always getting married. Two years after Abla and Yusef's wedding, my uncle Khaled had his own, and our family spared no expense for the celebration. There were over five hundred people gathered at the Intercontinental Hotel, spilling out of the ballroom and onto a terrace that overlooked the city. Palm trees glowed like firecrackers, and fake swans and floating flowers slid across a swimming pool, lit up by thousands of twinkling lights.

I spent most of the night with Omar, doing what we always did at weddings: sneaking food before we were supposed to, running through the hallways of the fancy hotel. As the older adults began to leave—signaling the beginning of the *real* party—we begged our parents to let us stay. When we saw a group of twenty or thirty guests gathering around Khaled and his new wife, Omar grabbed my arm.

"Let's go!" he said.

I wasn't sure where we were going, but I was happy to follow these young adults, mostly men, as they escorted the bride and groom through the hotel hallways, singing and clapping all the way. No one seemed concerned about the noise and the other hotel guests. Was this a different version of the zaffeh I didn't know about?

Finally, the party came to a stop outside of a guest room at the end of a long hallway. The bride and groom turned to their friends, smiled knowingly, and then disappeared into their suite. The crowd roared. I stood on my toes, trying to see what all the fuss was about, but all I could see was the closed door.

"What is happening?" I asked my cousin.

"Just wait!" Omar smiled.

Five minutes went by. The men sang a song that they all seemed to know by heart. They chanted. They shouted. They clapped. If anyone on this floor of the hotel had been asleep, they weren't anymore.

And then the door opened, but only a sliver. From inside, a white sheet came tumbling out of the dark. I jumped up and down trying to peer over shoulders, using Omar's for support. One of the men in the front of the group took hold of the sheet. He found the corners with his fingers and held it up high, displaying the sheet like a victory flag. Just as I saw it—a red stain piercing the white cotton—the crowd roared with approval.

"What is that?"

"She was a virgin!" Omar said happily.

"A virgin? How do you know?"

Omar smirked and opened his mouth to explain, but suddenly it hit me.

"Stop! Never mind."

I was dumbfounded. Every person outside that room knew the exact moment the bride lost her virginity, what should have been the most private moment of her life. What if the sheet hadn't been bloody? What would the crowd have done then? In that moment, I wished to be curled up under one of those tables, woken up by my father carrying me to the car.

Then something else struck me. Something even more

disturbing. One day soon, I would be the girl in that room.

I would let them all down. Maybe not tomorrow, maybe not the next day. But soon, Jiddo Riyad and Taytay, my mother and father, Abla and Omar, they would know the truth. And it was far worse than not being a virgin. For so long I thought I could pretend to like skirts and makeup and boys, pretend to be the kind of girl everyone wanted me to be.

But now I knew—there was a limit to pretending. Eventually, they would need proof I couldn't give them.

Weddings changed for me that night. They were no longer magical, whimsical celebrations. They were barbaric, suffocating rituals.

I had prayed for Allah to make me different, and he hadn't. Maybe it had been in my hands all along.

CHAPTER 7
KILL OR BE KILLED

WHEN MY PARENTS were first married, they struggled to get pregnant. After a couple years of trying, my mother, feeling overwhelmed by the pressure, visited a fortune-teller, a Bedouin woman who claimed she could see someone's future by studying the coffee grounds left at the bottom of their mug. She told my mother not to worry; she would conceive soon, and even better, it would be a boy. My mother was thrilled, and less than a year later, she gave birth to me, a girl.

This was a brilliant business strategy for the fortune-teller. She told my mom what she wanted to hear, what any woman in the Arab world would want to hear. If all this struggle to deliver a child meant that my mother might only have one, of course she would want that child to be a boy. After all, a boy would be the one who carried on the family name, who would be doted upon and served. He would stand at the front of the mosque, lead companies and countries.

Girls couldn't do those things. We were considered quieter, weaker, not as smart. The best we could do was to stay at home, support the family, do the doting and the serving. To stay out of the way. To be uncontroversial and unseen. Nobody told me this explicitly, or all at once, of course, but in lots of little messages delivered over the course of years.

Girls started helping with the housework around age six, while boys went outside to play. Girls had a curfew; boys didn't. Young men went away to England and the United States for college, but young women stayed in Jordan. Men passed their nationality on to their children and inherited the majority of the money when their parents died.

Let your brother sit in the front seat, I heard. *Never leave the house alone. Be nice to him, even if you don't like him in that way. Don't draw attention to yourself.*

Even though I had some kind of athletic practice nearly every day, I had to cover up my legs if I wasn't on the field. Even my very modest athletic shorts—the ones that nearly touched my knees—were considered inappropriate. And so I had to wear sweatpants over them (not pleasant in ninety-degree heat). Around our driver. Around the soldiers in the street. Around any man who might be tempted by my thick and hairy limbs. Girls and women, I learned as a teenager, should be invisible. And if we made ourselves visible, if we did something "wrong," we could never be "right" again.

No one told me about honor killings; they were everywhere. In stories that were passed down from generation to generation, in casual conversations in the streets. They were on the TV, in the newspapers, and the quiet chatter of adults in my grandparents' living rooms. I would pretend to play cards or read books, but I would listen. I would hear my uncles say, *She brought dishonor upon the family.*

Girls could bring dishonor in lots of ways—by tempting a man to have sex before marriage or committing adultery (men who partook in these activities, confusingly, did not dishonor their families). These things were not only against Islamic law; punishment for them was allowed under Jordanian law. Males from the woman's family were perfectly justified in hurting or killing a girl for dishonoring her family, and they wouldn't get in trouble or go to jail for doing so.

Even smaller offenses could provoke violent punishment. A girl could dishonor her family by dressing without modesty or simply looking at a man who wasn't her husband. One woman's eyes were gouged out by her husband because he thought he saw her looking at another man. Another woman was beaten to death in the middle of the street by her father, who pounded a brick into her head over and over as the neighbors watched silently. When he was done, his son, her brother, brought him a cup of tea and a chair to sit on as the girl's bloody body lay next to him. Her crime was going on a date.

Dishonor. That word took up permanent residence in my head. Sometimes I would look around the room and wonder which one of the men in my family would kill me if he knew about the shameful things I thought.

Omar? He was my cousin but also my best friend. The boy who climbed trees with me and snuck into Taytay's kitchen to steal food not meant for us. Omar wouldn't hurt me—other than the time he encouraged me to drink a concoction we made from my uncle's chemistry set—no, not Omar; he had my back. I just couldn't imagine it.

My brothers? But *I* was the one who beat up Ali and Saeed; I was stronger. And yeah, we fought, but we would never harm each other.

Khalo Khaled? My uncle who tickled us until we couldn't breathe, who rolled his eyes back into his head and plodded around pretending to be a zombie? Khalo couldn't kill anybody.

Maybe, I reasoned, honor killings didn't happen in families like ours. Or maybe they just hadn't happened yet.

THERE WASN'T ANYTHING special about the day I tried to kill myself. It was sunny and warm, a school night near the end of my ninth-grade year. I had just turned fifteen. My parents were out, one of the rare evenings when my brothers and I ate dinner just the three of us. Afterward, Ali and I got in a fight and I lost my temper. We fought a lot, but this fight felt like too much. Everything I had been holding inside—Jumana, Prince Talal, my uncle's wedding, the fear of dishonoring my family, and the certainty that one day I would—refused to stay buried for another second longer.

I had been envisioning my own death for months. I wished for a car accident, or for a car to hit me while I was on my bike. Sometimes I thought about tipping into traffic while I was riding—no one would know that I did it on purpose. In Islam, suicide is the greatest sin, but I wasn't going to heaven anyway. There wouldn't be forty virgins waiting on me. What was the point in hanging around if I knew how this was going to end?

The pain pills were left over from when I had torn a knee ligament playing basketball. The other bottles I took from my mother's bathroom vanity. I cradled them against my stomach on my way down the hall, making sure the pills didn't rattle as I walked back to my bedroom and shut the door.

I had chosen the smallest room when my parents added the second floor to our house, the room with the most windows. Everything fit perfectly—my desk was tucked between two windows; on top a pen, a pencil, a metal ruler, and an eraser lay in perfect, parallel lines. The built-in bookshelves housed a tidy display of trophies and certificates and a collection of books that I had meticulously arranged. If any of them were out of place, I would know. Behind my bed hung posters of Bon Jovi and the Pet Shop Boys, and two books were the only things I kept on my nightstand.

That night, as I sat on my bed with the bottles of pills in my hands, I studied my belongings, lit up by the evening sun reflected in the mirrored closet doors. My eyes lingered on the trophies and awards. Some were for academic achievements; others were for athletic accomplishments. But they were all lies, I thought. Everyone thought I was this perfect kid, but I wasn't. If people knew the truth, they wouldn't speak to me or cheer me on at games or give me awards.

The pills tickled my throat but went down surprisingly easy with just a glass of water. I felt resolved. I felt calm. I set the bottles on the nightstand and then lay back on the yellow-and-blue bedspread, the pillows the maid had probably fluffed that morning. I closed my eyes and waited to fall permanently asleep.

Most of the details of the hours between when I closed my eyes in my bedroom and when I opened them in the hospital are lost to me forever. I know that Ali had come to apologize when he found me and the empty bottles. I know that my parents had rushed home, and I guessed that my father carried me to the car and then drove me to the hospital, just ten minutes away. A fullness in my throat and the acrid taste in my mouth was the only evidence that my stomach had been pumped.

When I opened my eyes and saw a hospital room appear beyond my blanketed feet, I was confused. I felt like I was underwater; sounds were garbled, and my vision smudged. Why was I here? I certainly hadn't expected to wake up in heaven, but this didn't look like hell either. My parents were there, one on each side of me. They talked softly, but I struggled to make sense of their words. A doctor came in; he said something about a "psychologist." But then he and my father walked into the hallway together and when they came back, I was being discharged instead. The sun was blooming on the horizon as I leaned my head against the glass of the back seat window. The scenery passed in slow motion.

At home, my mother walked with me upstairs to my room. She pulled down the still-made bed. She didn't say anything as I crawled in; she just sat, perched there on the edge. And then Abla was there, and then Taytay, too. They formed a circle around me.

"You're a donkey," Abla said, swatting me playfully. My mother and grandmother smiled, coaxing me to smile back.

We sat there for a long time together. No one saying anything about what had happened. Abla and my mom just rubbed my legs and shoulders and tried to make me laugh, my head cradled in Taytay's lap, her fingers lightly scratching my scalp. I felt completely detached from my body, like I was watching the whole thing happen from above. Eventually, they left, and I fell into a deep, cavernous sleep. When I woke up, it was dark, and my parents were hosting a dinner party downstairs.

A few days later, after I had gone back to school and the scratchy feeling in my throat had faded, my parents told me there was someone to see me in the living room. "You can talk to him," they said, and then sent me in alone.

The man sat on one of the couches, his legs crossed and a briefcase at his feet. He wore white socks and shiny dress shoes. His hair was so coated in gel it looked like a plastic helmet on his head. I felt skeptical of this nerdy Dracula as I took the couch opposite him.

"Why did you do it?" he asked, leaning slightly forward in his seat. *How are you? My name is* . . . might have been a better approach. If I couldn't tell my own family, how was I supposed to tell someone I had never met?

"I don't know," I said, keeping my eyes on those dress shoes. He must have polished them that morning; they were exceptionally shiny.

But I did know. I did it because I didn't see any other options. Because I couldn't—just *couldn't*—live the life that lay in front of me: a few years at a local university before my mother found me a husband, a man I would be expected to marry and have children—and a bloody sheet—with. I did it because I knew for certain that if I didn't do it myself, I was going to die anyway.

And yet here I was. Alive. Sitting across from a stranger in my parents' house. Why was I alive?

I ASKED TO stay with Taytay for a while.

"It will be quieter there," I told my parents, who looked relieved to see me go. If anyone could reach me, it was her.

Taytay's house *was* quiet, but it was more than that. At Taytay's I could be myself. While my world was constantly changing—everyone else was growing up, dating, getting married, becoming the person they were expected to be—at Taytay's the world stood still. Or at least it did for me. I would shell beans and climb fruit trees and sit in her kitchen for hours. The outside world never infiltrated her sanctuary.

Taytay welcomed me with open arms and folded me into her daily life with ease. When Abed would drop me off from school or practice, she'd already be in the kitchen working on dinner. We'd chop and stir together, talk about our days. After the meal, we'd burrow into the couch, where I could work on homework or watch TV. Sometimes, aunts, uncles, or Lana and Omar came from the apartment upstairs to eat or play cards.

Sometimes I would ask Taytay if she would ever marry again.

"I am a fat old lady." She would laugh. "Who will marry me?"

"I will find you a husband," I'd say, knowing Taytay would never remarry and that I wouldn't like it if she did.

"I have my children and my grandchildren. That is all that I need."

Taytay also had Allah. She was rarely without her masbahah, the Islamic rosary that she'd wrap around her hand and wrist. To say the masbahah, you'd choose one of Allah's ninety-nine names and repeat it silently to yourself, over and over. Sometimes, Taytay would be so focused on her chanting she appeared tranced, and I knew not to talk to or bother her. During afternoon and evening prayers, Taytay would sit at the foot of her bed, toward the window that faced Mecca. With a white head covering, golden sunlight streaming in around her, she looked like an angel. She never invited me to prayer; she just led by example. As I stood in the doorway to her bedroom and watched her perform the prayer rituals of our faith, prayer seemed beautiful again, and I wanted to take part in it again even if I had to wear the white head covering.

Just like she was good at getting me to pray and making it seem like it was my idea, my grandmother could get me to open up without cajoling or asking probing questions. One minute we'd be talking about my cousins or telling an old story, and the next I'd be spilling my guts. She never asked why I did what I did, but one day I found myself telling her as best I could.

"I'm not like the others." The look in my grandmother's eyes told me that she understood I wasn't talking about the kids at school, even though I had already told her about the girls who made fun of my clothes. "Do you think Allah makes mistakes?" I asked.

"Allah doesn't make mistakes," she said, shaking her head.

"But what if he made a mistake with me?"

Taytay's eyes looked pained, but she smiled. "Habibti, Allah did not make a mistake with you."

I decided to believe her. If I was a mistake, then Allah would have let me die. But he didn't. Maybe there was a reason for that. The thought felt like a sliver of light shooting through my body.

After a few weeks, I went back home. Taytay had obviously told my parents about my troubles at school, because soon my mom asked if I would like to transfer to the American Community School for tenth grade. She didn't ask why I didn't like my current school, or why I felt different or didn't have any friends; like me, she seemed to just want to pretend like my suicide attempt never happened. And I was perfectly fine with that.

The American Community School wasn't as prestigious as the Baccalaureate School, but the kids were from all over, and a few of my cousins were there. Besides them, no one would know anything about me; I could start over. I'd be Luma the athlete, Luma the best friend, Luma the normal girl. And magically—that's just what happened.

Almost everything I had loved about my British elementary school I found again in the American Community School. It was full of kids of every race and nationality, where being different made you normal. Most of the students had parents who worked at the US State Department, had moved around a lot, and understood what it was like to be the new kid.

Still, that first day involved the typical stomachache, anxiety about where to sit at lunch and what outfit to wear. (I had been wearing a uniform for five years; the decision over what to wear was overwhelming.) That morning, as students gathered on the lawn in front of school, sharing hugs and stories about summer break, I stayed close to my younger cousin Hala. When a couple of girls approached us, I assumed they were Hala's friends, but instead they spoke to me. "You're a Mufleh, right?"

My jaw tightened at the question. All I had wanted was a clean slate, to be a nobody, or at least not a Mufleh.

"You must be a good athlete, then," one of them said with a grin.

I stuttered a bit, my teeth unclenching with relief, as Hala replied for me, "She's better than *I* am!"

"I'm the captain of the volleyball team," the girl went on. "You're going to play volleyball."

"Oh, I don't know how to play volleyball—"

Hala elbowed me gently in the rib. "She'd love to."

Within a few months, I was popular enough to be on student council. I had a group of friends like the kind I had once envied Abla for. We hung out after practice at the Chili House, a local fast-food joint, eating hot dogs and spaghetti. The girls told me about the boys they wanted to date; the boys told me about the girls they wanted to make out with. I listened a lot and talked very little. I was a confidante, a sounding board, an alibi in case their parents got suspicious. It was a relief to just be quiet.

I rooted for the couples who broke boundaries, who dated despite being from different classes, countries, or religions. As all my friends had their *firsts*—their first kisses, first dates, first dances—I felt only small pangs of curiosity. All of these firsts seemed thrilling, but also stressful. Instead, I convinced myself to feel grateful for the things I did have: these friendships, the chance to start over. I started to think of the girl who had swallowed all those pills as a different person, a different Luma.

Everything was going so well. And then the war started.

CHAPTER 8
INVASIONS

THAT SUMMER BEFORE I started at the American school, we were in Phuket, Thailand, at a seaside resort. A large group of us were traveling together—aunts, uncles, and cousins from both sides of the family—and the beach was the grand finale of our month in Thailand. But when news broke of the invasion, the men gathered around the TV like birds at a feeder, completely unmoved by the lure of swimming, snorkeling, or skiing in the turquoise water that stretched out below the balcony.

When our parents decided to cut our trip short and head back to Jordan, I was annoyed more than anything. War was normal, I thought. Sure, this one involved countries that shared a border with us, but Saddam Hussein had been killing people for decades, and wars over oil were nothing new. Why were we making a big deal? What was different about this time?

. . .

SADDAM HUSSEIN WAS a fixture, another Middle Eastern dictator I saw on TV and in headlines. Some Jordanians loved him for his Arab bravado and the cheap oil he sold to our country. Others despised him; it was well known that Hussein had gassed his own people to keep them from speaking out against the regime. One of my father's friends, a top advisor in Hussein's government, had died in a mysterious helicopter crash after publicly objecting to some of the dictator's methods.

Iraqis and Kuwaitis had a long history of conflict, and Hussein had invaded Kuwait so that he could take control of the country's large oil reserves to help pay off or cancel the debt that Iraq owed Kuwait. I liked to call this "dictator logic."

I thought Hussein was a jackass, but no more than the others: Assad in Syria, the monarchy in Saudi Arabia, men who reveled in power while their citizens suffered. These monsters won support by appearing big and brave, tough enough to stand up to extremists. But in reality, I thought, they were the extremists. Sadistic, narcissistic, and ruthless—especially when it came to their own people.

BACK IN AMMAN, the city looked different. There were more people in the streets, their faces worried and weary. They held suitcases, bags, and babies. They had fled from Kuwait, but they were Palestinians who had never been given Kuwaiti citizenship. Refugees twice over.

Seeing them I felt an impulse to welcome them somehow. We Arabs pride ourselves on hospitality, on feeding our visitors well and giving them the best bed in the house. You would never find a guest crammed onto a pull-out couch in the Middle East. I wanted to extend this kindness to those forced out from Kuwait somehow. It was one small thing I could do in an otherwise helpless situation.

I asked my dad if I could serve dinner to the Palestinians passing into Amman. He rolled his eyes, but he went out and bought the rice and meat I would need.

I told Abed that we were going to serve food from the Ping-Pong table in the backyard. He said, "I will get the people." Our home was not on a main street, so I was worried that no one would find it. But Abed delivered.

All afternoon, Palestinians arrived. They smiled, they were friendly, they stood around the backyard eating and chatting. It almost felt like a big family barbecue. Meanwhile, I walked uninterrupted laps between the kitchen and the yard, delivering full trays of fruit, refilling the tea, and replenishing paper plates and disposable utensils. More and more people came. They leaned over the table, putting their weight on its flimsy legs while they filled their dishes.

Suddenly, one side of the table collapsed, sending tin-foil trays of food crashing into the ground. For a moment, we were all dumbfounded and quiet: me, Abed, all the guests in the yard with their paper plates of rice and lamb and fruit.

I don't remember who giggled first, but soon we were all laughing. At least we still had the other half of the table.

It felt so good to help.

THE NEWS WAS always on. At Jiddo Riyad's, the television boomed from its place in the center of the living room. At Taytay's, the TV whispered from the corner. But in both houses, it was a constant, an ever-present monologue of trouble. Agitated by the unrest in the region and sudden influx of refugees, Jordanians were growing unhappy about their own government's dysfunction: the constant price fixing, the poor education system, the country's reliance on foreign aid. New political parties were sprouting up, trying to take advantage of the unrest. The Muslim Brotherhood won a bunch of seats in parliament, promoting a return to religious-based law instead of the mix of religious and secular law that Jordan currently relied on. Many Jordanians had seen the extreme rules put into place in Iran—where secret police used torture and executions to keep people compliant—and didn't want that to happen in Jordan. We were never going to separate church and state, but we could at least hope for a moderate church.

But it was hard to know what was really going on. The censors may have been bad at monitoring American television shows, but state-sponsored news kept a tight filter on information coming in and out of the country. Back then, without the internet or social media, this was much easier to do. A couple times during my childhood, my dad sat my brothers and me down in front of the Israeli news channel and told us to try to learn Hebrew. *Not all news is the same,* he said.

During the war, CNN became available in Jordan and changed everything. Never before had we had access to so much news—so much different news—so many hours of the day. Now we could watch in real time as Hussein made threats to attack Israel, a move that would put Jordan right in the middle of the fighting. But CNN cost money; most Jordanians couldn't afford it. And so they continued to rely on the state-controlled TV, seeing and hearing what the government wanted them to see and hear.

THE AIR RAID sirens began to practice; their screaming was so loud you could feel it in your teeth. On the TV, men demonstrated how to put on a gas mask. In school, we learned how to put them on. One day my father gathered my brothers and me and explained that in the event of a chemical attack, the safest place to be was in the pool outside, where the water would protect us from the gas. I thought of us in the pool, our heads peeking above water. How long would we be there? Would we have time to change into bathing suits or would we jump in in our clothes?

By October, duct-tape X's began appearing in windows throughout Amman. If Amman were to be bombed, the tape was supposed to prevent the glass from exploding into the house. When I asked my dad if we would tape our windows, he told me no. "We are not scared," he said. It didn't make sense to me. If something so small and simple might protect us—like a bike helmet or a seat belt—why wouldn't we take advantage of it? Why would we pretend everything was normal when it was not? Or maybe he knew that tape was not going to protect us; we needed full body armor, not just a helmet.

AFTER OUR TRADITIONAL potluck Thanksgiving, the school closed as the American embassy evacuated its staff, including their children, my new friends at the American school. Lots of teachers went back to their countries of origin, too. Everyone was leaving. The Jordanian government issued a curfew and set limits to how much people could move around the country. Our lives became very small. I read books and played cards with my cousins. In the evenings, we would walk over to Taytay's and she would cook us a feast. We grabbed on to any semblance of normalcy we could have.

I had grown up around war, but now I was in the middle of one. Our days were filled with a terrifying monotony, with no end in sight.

WE WERE BORED teenagers tired of being at home with our families. We wanted things to be normal again. One of my new friends from school, Amin, called and said his driver would take a few us to the Dead Sea for the afternoon. It was winter; warmish, but still sweater weather. We didn't care—we wanted to go anyway.

I told my parents I would be at Amin's house, a place I could walk to from home. It took us about an hour to drive to the sea, where a ribbon of water carved through the desert. The Dead Sea is only about ten miles at its widest point, and the hills of Israel loomed hazy in the distance.

We rolled up our pant legs and waded into the still water, feeling the salt burn in the small cuts we didn't even know we had. On the beach, a layer of saline turned chalky on our skin. It felt so good to be together and out of Amman.

We had gotten back in the car when the sirens started blaring. A spine-chilling wail of a sound. All together we looked up through the windshield to see the Scud missiles fly over us. Iraq was bombing Israel.

There were lots of reasons for this. Hussein realized attacking Kuwait made him look bad: a big country attacking a tiny one. So he attacked Israel hoping to lure the United States, an outspoken ally of Israel, into the war. If the rest of the Middle East saw Hussein standing up to Israel and the United States, he hoped they would line up behind him. Impeccable dictator logic.

My childhood was surrounded by tanks and soldiers and guns and swords (albeit the ones I saw were for slicing wedding cakes and dancing), but I had never seen a missile. Time thickened; sound grew fuzzy. I watched them sail through the sky, somehow fast and yet slow enough that I could read ALLAHU AKBAR—"God is the greatest"— painted in thick paint on the missile large enough for us to read.

Someone in the car screamed.

The driver followed the chaotic mass of vehicles that beelined to a bomb shelter carved into a nearby hill. We stood and waited. No one said much, and I was surprised by how calm I felt. It was almost laughable—the one time I snuck out of the house: Scud missiles. It would be a while before I did that again.

When I got home, my dad was stationed in front of CNN.

"Iraq bombed Israel," he said.

"Really?" I pretended to be surprised.

WHEN SADDAM HUSSEIN refused to pull his troops out of Kuwait, America did get involved. A huge percentage of the world's oil supply was at stake. I was glad about this; my father was not. Many Arabs were not; they didn't want the West meddling in their business. I wanted the United States to get rid of the tyrants that we never could. Not a lot of people felt the way I did about American involvement, but, really, all of us just wanted the same thing. Someone else to save us—a brutal dictator or Western liberators. I just happened to prefer the latter.

When the US began dropping bombs, we listened to the American journalists on CNN say, almost serenely, "Something is happening outside . . . The skies over Baghdad have been illuminated."

We went outside to listen for bombs and look for flashes even though Iraq's capital city is hours from Jordan's. All we could see was stars.

IN FEBRUARY, A few teachers and administrators came back to open our school. They were my heroes. Believing so much in their students that they would do anything, including ignoring their embassy's travel advisory, to make sure we could continue the school year. There were so few adults that students had to make the morning announcements, cover classes for younger students, and help supervise lunch.

On a Monday, we found the white walls of the school marred with red paint: SADDAM WILL WIN! and DEATH TO THE ALLIES and ALLAHU AKBAR.

The next day, US Marines were stationed outside the school and the Jordanian guards were gone.

PEOPLE IN KUWAIT said that Iraqi soldiers had taken babies from incubators and left them to die. People in Iraq said the US bombed the only baby formula plant in Baghdad. People in the US argued that it was a biological weapons facility dressed up to look like baby formula plant. Once again, it was hard to figure out who was telling the truth.

The TV showed the faces of American soldiers who had been held as POWs. Their lips were fat, and their eyelids were purple.

The baby formula story gnawed at me. The busted faces of the POWs haunted me. I told my family that I would fast until the war was over.

"What, you think you're Gandhi now?" my brothers and cousins teased.

The next night at Taytay's I didn't come to the dinner

table when it was time to eat. Taytay found me on the couch, wrapped me up in her arms, and with her chin on my forehead, she said, "Habibti, this is not how you stop wars."

I lasted three more days before I broke my fast. This Gandhi shit was no joke.

THE WAR ENDED as abruptly as it began. At the end of February, Iraqi forces set fire to hundreds of oil wells in Kuwait and fled the country. The US declared victory but left Saddam Hussein in power. That didn't seem like victory to me, especially for the people in Iraq. Nothing had changed; the same people were in power, and those who had been forced to leave their homes were simply forgotten.

The duct-tape X's began disappearing from the windows like curtains thrown open. Tennis season started. Our hearts skipped back to their normal rhythm, and life went on, just like it always had.

CHAPTER 9
A WORD FOR WHAT I AM

DURING MY SOPHOMORE tennis season, I mostly played singles. The tennis court was the only place I performed alone. I liked that, liked that my success and failure were completely my own. I knew how to carry a team. But I certainly never let a team carry me. I played injured. I practiced more often and harder than anyone else, every day, all the time. In exchange, team sports gave me a group to fold myself into. A community. On the other hand, tennis gave me the chance to laser in on the only person I could truly count on—myself.

We had tennis practice every day after school, and most days, while my teammates hung out trading snacks and gossip in the interim, I would sneak away to the library for twenty minutes to myself.

The American Community School had a great library, all dark wood and hidden nooks hemmed in by bookshelves.

That year I was tearing through Dean Koontz and Stephen King books—which I loved for their ability to transport me to another reality far, far away from my own—and usually I would find a place on the floor to get through as many pages as possible before practice. Some days, I would browse the magazines instead. The library offered tons of American magazines for all the kids missing home. As I studied them, I began to notice that the American versions weren't exactly the same as the Jordanian versions my parents received, which included different stories more relevant to Arabs and left out anything that was considered inappropriate in the region, like sex and democracy. The magazines at the library—inked on the back with a US embassy or US State Department stamp—were dispatches from the Western world.

One afternoon, flipping through the magazines, I noticed that the American version of *Time* had tennis player Martina Navratilova's name in it. I was a Steffi Graf fan, but I took the magazine to my spot on the floor anyway.

There were a few reasons I preferred Graf over Navratilova. Graf was the young up-and-comer, the underdog. She seemed quiet and humble, whereas Navratilova was always arguing with the referee and making a scene. I also knew that Navratilova had defected from her home country of Czechoslovakia to play in the US. At the time, I didn't understand that the communist regime in

Czechoslovakia was trying to force Navratilova—the best tennis player in the world—to stop playing in Western countries, where most of the biggest tournaments were held, a move that would have effectively ended her career. All I knew was that the US was full of great athletes; I couldn't understand why Navratilova wouldn't want to represent her country, to make her people proud.

I flipped through the thin pages until I found the article. Just enough fluorescent light pushed through the gaps in the bookshelves so that I could read:

She transformed sports for women by taking on the training discipline of men—lifting weights, running sprints, following a rigid carbohydrate-loaded diet. She emphasized mental preparation as much as physical . . .

I nodded my head in approval; I could picture the shelf of trophies in my room. I knew a little something about devotion and discipline. I kept reading.

Perhaps her most lasting legacy is having lived as an open homosexual . . .

I bolted upright; my heart thumped against my chest. The room buzzed with a completely new sensation as I reread the words.

An open homosexual . . .

Tears fell onto the glossy pages; my body moved with the breath I felt I had been holding my entire life.

Other gay superstars duck questions, solicit a conspir-
acy of silence, make marriages of convenience. . . .

Suddenly, I was Navratilova's biggest fan. Everything that had once turned me off about her began to make sense. She wasn't argumentative; she was authentic. She wasn't unruly; she was unapologetic. Not just a superstar—
a gay superstar.

I wasn't the only one. There were others. Allah hadn't forgotten to install a piece of me on his assembly line of people; the doctor who delivered me hadn't screwed up. All along, I had known that this feeling—this being *gay*, I could now call it—wasn't in my control, but that had done nothing to ease the terrible shame of it. And here was Martina Navratilova. Wildly successful. Worshipped. Unashamed.

A little over a year ago, I had tried to kill myself because the future I saw ahead of me was unbearable. Now, for the first time, I could envision a completely different kind of future. In it, I could be happy and successful. Fully me. Like Navratilova (without the Wimbledon title, unfortunately). I just needed to get to America.

I pulled my knees to my chest and used them to wipe my eyes. A few minutes later, I got up, put the magazine back on the rack, and headed to practice.

THERE WAS NEVER a question that I would go to college. My parents had sent me to the best schools in Jordan for a reason. And it certainly wasn't out of the question that I could go abroad after high school. Both my parents had: my dad attended college in upstate New York, and my mother went to finishing school in England. Getting to the US wouldn't be impossible, but it certainly wasn't a given.

Out of my small army of cousins, only one female had ever gone to the US. Zina attended Georgetown to study linguistics. When she did, she sparked a debate in the family. One side said that Zina was brilliant, the top student in her high school class—of course she should go. The other side said that Washington, DC, was too far, that American men couldn't be trusted, that young girls needed protection.

Many of the women in my family, like Aunt Abla, attended the University of Jordan, a perfectly acceptable college. The ones who went abroad almost always went to England. England was close, a six-hour flight. We had lots of extended family in London who could keep an eye on the girls and be there quickly in case of trouble. But for me, going to England would be more of the same—pretending, keeping up a charade in front of family before it was time to go back to Jordan and get married. To be fully myself, I knew, I needed to be all alone. I needed to go to America.

America didn't just promise anonymity. The words *freedom* and *equality* called out to me, two things I knew that Jordan could never offer. If it was good enough for Martina, it was good enough for me. My spotless transcript and American high school diploma would be a start, but first I would need my parents' blessing.

I began dropping hints about my desire to go to the US. Sometimes, I would bring the globe to the couch where my mother sat reading her magazines.

"Where's the very opposite of Jordan?" I would say loud enough for her to hear, tracing my finger up and over the North Pole and down the other side until it stopped in Hawaii.

My mother always took the bait. "You will miss me, habibti!"

Slowly, my parents opened the negotiation. The East Coast, they said, would be acceptable. Preferably Boston, where there was a large Arab community and some of my male cousins studied at schools like Tufts, Harvard, and Boston University. My father, who memorized college rankings as if there would be an exam, insisted that it would be an elite school or no school at all. That's the way it was for girls. Boys could go to any college and call it an achievement. Girls had to overachieve to go anywhere at all. Sometimes I thought the sky-high standards were supposed to discourage me from trying, but other times I believed my parents were preparing me for the challenges ahead. Either way, their expectations for my success only made me want it more.

Haverford or Swarthmore, my father suggested. Nostalgic for his own years in the rural landscapes of upstate New York, he said St. Lawrence or Cornell could be good options. When he proposed an all-women's school like Smith or Wellesley, I put my foot down. In Jordan, all-women's schools were substandard. Those schools were certainly inferior, I told him. I wasn't going all that way just to be a second-class citizen—again.

In the end, I set my sights on Brown University. An Ivy League school on the East Coast would satisfy my parents. From the brochures, Brown seemed rigorous but not stuffy, renowned but not enormous. By the time my junior year began, the plan seemed set in stone. I would graduate, I would move to Providence, Rhode Island, and I would be free. All I needed was an acceptance letter.

CHAPTER 10
OUT OF MY LEAGUE

BETWEEN SPORTS AND student council and yearbook and all the other extracurriculars I was cramming onto my transcript, my days were full. Even if dating had been a possibility for me, I wouldn't have had time. Plus, I could live vicariously through my friends, many of whom seemed to devote *all* their time to the opposite sex. The girls fantasized about feelings, true love, while the guys just fantasized, and I nodded along to it all.

One of the places where their romantic dramas played out was in the gym. Our teams weren't coed, but our practices were. In the bleachers before and after practices, I would join the huddle of guys sitting around commenting on girls' bodies. After practice there would be a community open gym for the US embassy staff and expats, so the guys would find an excuse to stay late and ogle the young American women who were playing.

In the middle of the season, my basketball coach mentioned that the embassy was looking for high school students to play pickup games, since after the war many of them now lacked enough players to make full teams. She asked that our team stick around for a scrimmage after practice; it would be good for us to play against bigger, stronger athletes.

About halfway through the scrimmage, I began to feel like someone was watching me. When I turned my head to see who it was, a woman with brown, wavy hair quickly looked away. I recognized her as one of the women the boys were commenting on as she ran up and down the court.

"She's pretty," one had said.

"She's hot," another corrected.

"I'd do her."

"She wouldn't do you." I tried putting the guys in their place when their fantasies and chauvinism got out of control.

"She would."

"She wouldn't even look at you."

"Well, I get hard looking at her."

"Grow up."

Was this the high school version of my elementary school conversation with Justin and Michael? I had become one of the guys, but even for me, this was a little much.

A few minutes later, I felt her eyes on me again. Maybe she had heard us. Maybe she was going to confront me. But this time, when I looked over, she didn't turn away—she smiled. Amin was right, she *was* hot. Something in my chest fluttered, but I quickly shook it off. This woman was almost twice my age; surely, she wasn't looking at me like *that*.

After the game, I found a spot on the bleachers to change out of my gym shoes and pull on some sweatpants. As I untied my laces, two long, muscular legs appeared in front of me. I looked up to see that they belonged to the woman who had been staring at me.

"Good game," she said, with that smile again. It was a nice smile, I thought, eager and bright. As she reached down to squeeze my shoulder, I noticed her damp hair, her flushed skin.

"I'm Susan."

"Luma," I said, hoping my face wasn't as red as it felt.

From then on, I finished my homework before practice so I could play with the adults, often on a team playing Susan's. Sometimes we would play man-to-man defense, and I'd get to guard her (a little difficult; she was four inches taller). Sometimes we'd play zone defense instead, and even though we would be on opposite ends of the court (because of our height difference), I could still feel the weird energy between us.

A few weeks after that first game, Susan offered to give a few of us a ride home. I took the front seat and helped her navigate the dark streets of Jabal Amman as we dropped one of my teammates off and then the other.

"Where are you from?" I asked when I was the last one remaining in the car.

"Houston," she answered. "We came here for my husband's job."

Husband, I thought, *so I* had *imagined the thing between us.*

We drove mostly in awkward silence, except for the directions I gave. Five minutes later, we were in front of my house.

"Thanks for the—" I began, shifting to collect my gym bag from between my feet.

"Wait," she said, grabbing my forearm.

"I am running late; my parents flip out when I don't come home on time."

"Have you ever watched *Witness*?"

"I don't like Michael Douglas."

"It's not Michael Douglas; it's Harrison Ford."

"Same thing. Two old farts with three facial expressions," I joked nervously. But she was the one acting nervous.

"Do you know what sexual tension is?"

"No. What is it?"

"You know what it is, and I think we have that between us."

I looked down at Susan's hand, still on my arm, and felt myself smile.

"Thanks for the ride," I said slowly, and got out of the car.

Before I went inside, I stood at the front door, taking deep breaths of air, trying to slow down my racing heart. I felt almost sick with anticipation. Was this happening? Was this happening *to me*? I had listened as many of my friends described these feelings, but I tried so hard to never imagine them for myself.

For days, I avoided Susan. I didn't know what I'd say if we talked, and I thought maybe if I played it cool, she'd want me more. I'd jump into the games she wasn't in. Sometimes I would skip the pickup games altogether, surprising my teammates who had never seen me opt out of practice. But I was only prolonging the inevitable.

A couple weeks after that ride home, there was a party for the basketball teams at the Embassy Club. I knew Susan would be there; all the adults we played pickup games with were coming to give us a big send-off before that weekend's tournament. A comradery had grown between the two groups. Moments into the party, I noticed Susan across the room and purposefully stayed close to my group of friends.

As the night was winding down, everyone started making other plans, including my ride, who ditched me to hang out with his girlfriend. Suddenly, I was standing alone, downing the rest of my soda and scanning the room for a plan B.

"I'll take you home," Susan, suddenly behind me, offered.

"No, it's okay. I don't want to be any trouble."

"Not a problem, I am taking Jake home. It's on the way."

"All right, then," I said, relieved that someone else would be in the car.

I didn't know what I was more afraid of, that these feelings were mutual or that I had completely misinterpreted our interactions. I thought about what had happened with Isabella and Jumana, and didn't want it to happen again.

As we drove, the three of us chatted about the upcoming tournament, the teams that would be traveling from the region to attend.

When Susan dropped Jake off, my heartbeat ratcheted up. A couple blocks later, she took her foot off the gas, pulling her car over to the curb and gently engaging the parking brake.

"This is not my house."

"Are you avoiding me?" Her brown eyes looked worried.

"No."

"Do you want to talk?"

"There's nothing to talk about," I said, and meant it.

"Are you sure?"

"Yes, I'm sure." I glanced at her legs. She was wearing a miniskirt. She was grinning when I looked back up. She leaned over. She kissed me.

In an instant, everything about my life felt changed, transformed. That kiss made me feel good, and I wanted more. I suddenly understood what all my friends had been saying about their own kisses, even if I would never be able to tell them about mine. No, I couldn't tell anyone about this. It would be my secret. Our secret.

Susan taught me things I didn't know existed. We did it

in the classrooms and in the gym, on the roof of the gym, in her car and in her house (when her husband wasn't home), Susan instructing me to go slow, to take my time, her fingers in my hair. Afterward, Susan would drive me home, stopping for shawarmas on the way. I was always famished after our time together.

It was so risky, but I convinced myself not to care. I'd waited so long. The magazine I'd found in the library taught me what this was called; Susan taught me how it felt.

All of the ways in which Susan was absolutely wrong for me, paradoxically, made her perfect. At thirty-two, she was closer to my mother's age than mine. But I liked that Susan was older; she knew exactly what she was doing and was more than willing to teach me how to do it, too. Because she was married, her husband employed by the embassy, it was crucial that our encounters stay top secret. I could be absolutely sure that Susan wouldn't tell anyone about us and that no one would ever find out. Plus, Susan was technically unavailable. There was no chance that this could turn into any kind of real relationship. That suited me fine. I was busy, I was going to Brown, I didn't need attachments.

Maybe somewhere, deep down, I knew it wasn't right. But that instinct was drowned out by the intoxicating notion that maybe I could be just like everyone else.

CHAPTER 11
I'VE GOT A FEELING

SUSAN AND I saw each other every week or so, often enough that our meetings became unremarkable. The thrill of the affair became mundane. We had chemistry, but not a lot in common. She liked to listen to Peter, Paul, and Mary; I preferred New Kids on the Block and Nirvana. She liked romance novels. I liked murder mysteries. Something that once seemed impossible—being with a woman—now seemed commonplace. After four months, I got bored. It no longer consumed me. Where once I would obsessively think and plan out every detail about the next time I would see her, I started dreading it. It blurred into the background of my life. As I began senior year, I was more focused on those other milestones I was set to check off: graduation, the college acceptance letter. I was committed to enjoying every second of it. Our school had slowly filled back up after the war, but my graduating class was still small, twenty-three instead of sixty-five, and we had become close.

The biggest event of the fall was the coed regional volleyball tournament, which, for the first time ever, was going to take place at the American Community School. We were usually overlooked because of our size and small facilities, but that year, the teams that had hosted us in the past—Cairo, Cyprus, Athens, Abu Dhabi, Dubai, Kuwait, Syria—were going to come to Jordan. We were ready to bask in the spotlight, showing everyone what our country had to offer. We planned a trip to the Dead Sea and an epic dance party to welcome everyone to Amman. We would play "Macarena" on repeat.

I met Julie at the airport, where I had gone with some of my teammates to pick up the players coming in from Egypt. I'm sure I was introduced to everyone there in the terminal, but the only person I remember meeting is her. Everything about Julie was perfect: her perfect American accent, her perfect teeth, her perfectly wavy, perfectly brown hair. I made sure we sat next to each other on the bus back to school.

"Are you a senior?" I asked, immediately regretting such a boring question.

"Yeah," Julie said, a little shyly, tucking a strand of hair behind her ear.

"Me too." For a moment, we both stared straight ahead without saying anything. Just as I began scolding myself for being so dull, Julie spoke.

"Where are you going to school next year?"

"Brown," I said, hoping to impress her. "What about you?"

"I think I am going to California or Oregon."

"That's far."

"I know, but there's this great school that I really want to go to. Reed College?" She looked over to see if I recognized the name.

"Isn't that a school for hippies?"

"Intellectual bohemians," she corrected me with playful irritation. Something in her eyes suggested that I had just passed a test. For the next thirty minutes, the conversation was effortless. We moved from Chaucer to Wilde, to Koontz to King, to Lennon and McCartney. We both thought Paul was the best Beatle and *Let It Be* was the best Beatles album. I couldn't decide whether it was more fun to congratulate each other on our good taste or tease each other when it didn't line up. Either way, I wished the ride would never end.

Julie must have felt the same. When we got back to the school, she followed me into the gym, where some of my teammates were already setting up for the dance— hanging streamers and arranging chairs around the room. When her friends asked if she wanted to go unpack together, Julie looked at me. "No, I'm going to stay and help." My stomach did three somersaults and a cartwheel.

Hours later, boys and girls began pouring into the gym. Soon, the dance floor was packed with bodies; chaperones stood in huddles along the perimeter, talking to each other and hardly paying attention. I looked around at all the sweaty, happy faces in the crowd. Tomorrow we would be rivals, but tonight we were friends—and potential hookups.

Julie grabbed my arm. "Let's go," she said, close enough to my ear so that I could hear her words above the music.

"Go where?"

"It's *your* school."

"You don't want to dance?"

"Not really." She shook her head playfully.

On the roof of the gym, the air was as thin and cool as strands of ribbon. I led Julie to the tennis courts and motioned for her to sit down. She did, putting her shoulder against mine. This all felt so easy, so normal. Julie was beautiful and smart—and my age. I thought about Susan with a twinge of regret. Was I with her because I thought no one my age would want to be with me? That only an older married woman would be attracted to me? Maybe my love life didn't have to be a shameful secret.

We were quiet for a few minutes, and then Julie pointed to the sky. "That's Pisces."

"I'm a Pisces," I said, looking up. "Where is it?"

Julie took my hand and lifted it to the sky, connecting each star of the constellation. After she traced the whole thing with our hands, she pulled us both down so that we were lying with our heads touching.

"I'm a Virgo," she said.

"Compatible?" I looked over at her.

"Very." Julie flipped onto her elbow and leaned toward me.

"Who's up here?" The voice came from the direction of the stairwell. I knew immediately it was Mr. Bates, a science teacher and one of the chaperones.

I sprung to my feet, dusting off the back of my pants. Julie did the same.

"It's just me, sir," I yelled. "I was showing Julie the tennis courts."

"Well, you shouldn't be up here," he said, now coming into view around an equipment locker.

Julie and I both offered another apology before scurrying toward the stairs.

Back at the dance, everyone was still lost in their own romantic conquests; no one had even noticed we were gone. Except for Mr. Bates.

That night, at home, I tossed and turned. Couldn't we fast-forward and skip this part? Couldn't it be morning already? I knew I needed to sleep to play my best in the morning, but if I slept, I couldn't think about Julie.

"Good morning." Julie looked as tired as I felt. "How are you?"

"Tired," I sighed with wide eyes. "Didn't get much sleep."

"Me neither," she said with a knowing lift of her eyebrows.

As if Julie couldn't be any more perfect, I learned, as I watched her first game, that she was the captain of her team *and* the leading scorer. A few times, after she served an ace, she looked over and gave me a satisfied smirk. Between games, we inhaled hot dogs together, making each other laugh so hard we almost spit out our drinks. Julie gave me the name of the family she was staying with, and we made plans to hang out that night.

I took her to a café I liked downtown, a hole-in-the-wall that served rotisserie chicken on paper plates.

"Is this your idea of a fancy dinner?" Julie joked.

"Are jeans your idea of a fancy outfit?" I retorted, and we both laughed.

We sat at a table on the sidewalk, the heat of the day finally burning off the concrete. The air smelled like car exhaust; the chicken fell off the bone. We dipped it in garlic sauce and licked our fingers. We guzzled lukewarm sodas out of glass bottles. We were ravenous.

After dinner, we got ice cream. Chocolate for me, strawberry for Julie. And then it was time to take her home.

Arm in arm, we walked from my car to the gate of her host family's home.

"When will I see you again?" she asked.

"I'm not sure—hopefully soon."

"Maybe you can come to Cairo over Christmas break?"

I knew that I couldn't, but still I said, "I'll try."

We hugged for a long time. As Julie pulled away, she reached into her purse and took out a folded-up piece of paper.

"Well, bye, Luma," she said as she handed me the paper.

"Bye, Julie."

When I got back in the car, I unfolded the note. In her perfect handwriting, Julie had written her address and—.

All these years I've been wandering around,
Wondering how come nobody told me
All that I was looking for was somebody
Who looked like you

I laughed and closed my eyes. I imagined Paul McCartney's throaty voice and Julie's pretty smile.

That night, as I lay awake in my bed for the second night in a row, I was surprised to feel happy. Not that Julie had left or that I would likely never see her again. Happy because the two days with Julie had made me feel something completely new and totally exhilarating—normal.

Maybe I would find someone like Julie at Brown.

CHAPTER 12
POMP AND CIRCUMSTANCE

I WORKED SO hard. Participated in every extracurricular I could feasibly fit into my schedule and studied endlessly for the SAT. I got a perfect score on my TOEFL exam, the exam that measures proficiency in English. It was the only time I ever did well on a standardized test. My guidance counselor, a short, serious man named Dr. Miller, assured me my chances of getting into Brown were good. I had some of the best letters of recommendation he had ever seen.

Only one person had their doubts—an old classmate of mine from the Baccalaureate School, a prince (yet another one), who had also applied to Brown.

"They only accept one Jordanian," he told me when we crossed paths at the Chili House.

"Why would they only accept one Jordanian?"

"They just do. And it's going to be me." His arrogance shouldn't have surprised me, but it did. A C student, this boy was average in everything he tried. Sure, he was royalty, but that wouldn't hold water at Brown, in America. Over there it wasn't about your title or who you knew, it was about merit. It was about hard work and earning what you got. He was in for a rude awakening, I thought. Wrong on every count.

My parents were out of town when the letter came. It was late afternoon in November; the sun slashed through a hazy sky. Abed had run errands, stopping by the post office on his way back. He smiled as he handed me the razor-thin envelope, unaware of the devastating news that it held.

When I flipped the envelope over and saw the return address, my heart sank. I knew what was in it. Large, thick packages were acceptance letters; standard-size, thin envelopes were rejections. Sure enough, the first lines read:

Dear Miss Mufleh,
    After carefully reviewing your application, we regret to inform you . . .

Immediately, I thought of the things I could have done differently, better. Model UN. Track and field. Speech and debate. Would it have mattered? Or did Brown simply see through all the flawless transcripts and flashy trophies? Maybe they knew what I had kept concealed from everyone else for so long—that I was damaged, unworthy.

I didn't think about where I was going, just got on my bike. Halfway through my frantic peddling, I realized I was on the way to Dr. Miller's house, down the street a few blocks. I knew where the teachers' apartments were; I had passed them on the way to my grandfather's countless times. The street was filled with embassy license plates.

Dr. Miller opened on the first knock, confused to see me at his door, my bike discarded on the driveway.

"What is the matter?" he asked, his hand on my shoulder, gathering me into the air-conditioned foyer. I handed him the letter and then let the tears come—great, torrential waves of tears. I had never been so emotional—or emotional at all—in front of someone, but what did it matter now?

After he scanned the first sentences of the letter, Dr. Miller soberly folded it back up and placed it on a table next to the door.

"This is why we made a backup plan—"

"There is no backup, it's only Brown." I heaved.

"You applied to a dozen schools. There will be more."

"They will all say no!"

"I told you Brown was the most selective."

I knew there was only one way to get Dr. Miller to fully understand what was at stake. I had to say it. I had to say the impossible thing, the words that had hidden in my hunched shoulders and clenched fists and feet that could never stay still. That had lingered, leering, at the edge of family dinners and school dances and shopping trips with my mother. That had haunted my sleep the way Jiddo Suheil heard bombs in his dreams. I had to tell him.

"I'm gay." It was the first time I said it out loud.

Dr. Miller got quiet; his eyes registering something that looked like fear. He understood. "You will get out. We will get you out," he said firmly.

I didn't believe him. I had played by the rules. I had done everything that everyone told me to do. But it wasn't enough. *I* wasn't enough. I never would be.

Dr. Miller wanted me to stay, to have some water and sit for a while, but at some point during our conversation, I had begun thinking about something back at the house. My father's gun.

I was back home in less than five minutes. I didn't bother to take off my shoes, just strode into my parents' bedroom, flung open the closet, and knelt down. The hems of my mother's dresses grazed the top of the safe.

My father had reminded me of the combination to the safe nearly every time he and my mother left town. If there was an emergency—go to the safe and get money, he said. If there was ever a reason to flee, riots or war—go to the safe and get the jewelry. We had never talked about the gun that was lying there between the rolled-up wads of bills and my mother's jewelry box.

I picked up the gun, pulling it into my chest and curling

my spine toward my knees. I made an inventory of the ways I had been so stupid: for thinking I could ever be with someone like Julie, for thinking I would get into Brown or out of Jordan. It had been three years since I had swallowed those pills, but this darkness, this familiar dread, was like pulling on an old sweater and finding that it still fit perfectly after all this time.

There had been small openings of hope—the magazine in the library, Julie, Brown. But now the door was slamming shut. I was going to die anyway.

The muzzle was cold and sharp against my head. No last words, no last thoughts, no last breath. Just a determined squeeze of my index finger.

Nothing happened. The gun was locked. It was as if all my despair and desperation had slammed up against a brick wall. I put the weapon back in the safe and closed the door.

A few days later I learned that my former classmate, the prince, had been accepted to Brown.

THE ACCEPTANCE LETTERS did come. Haverford, Swarthmore, Hobart and William Smith. My father chose for me. He couldn't wait to introduce me to the rolling hills and valleys of upstate New York, where I would live as a freshman at Hobart and William Smith. As winter gave way to spring, my parents began planning my graduation party and booking flights to the United States; all the while I felt only a dull sense of relief.

Even the pressure to choose a date to prom hardly registered with me. I was surprised when my friend Yaseen, a boy I had known since the ninth grade, asked me to go with him. Extra surprised because I thought that if there was anyone else who was like me, who was gay, it was Yaseen. Though he dated girls, talked about girls incessantly, I just had a feeling I couldn't quite put my finger on.

"Why won't you go with me?" Yaseen asked when I turned him down.

You know exactly why, I wanted to tell him. Instead, I just told him he was being ridiculous. In the end, I went with David, a short, scrawny sophomore.

Graduation took place on a Thursday afternoon in May. I sat onstage with my classmates, facing an audience comprised of teachers, staff, families; even the janitors and bus drivers were there. I found my mother's face in the crowd. Her rouged cheeks moved as she gave me a wink. Taytay was next to her, a floral hijab loose around her hair. Inam bounced happily on Abla's knee.

Valedictorian went to Khalid, a wildly smart boy who had never broken a single rule in his life. As he bowed to accept his medal from the headmaster, I wondered with a detached curiosity if the distinction would have gotten me into Brown. Consumed by my own morbid thoughts,

I was jolted back to the present by the sound of my name.

"This award is for a student who is a good representative of their own country, with a positive attitude toward the life and culture of others," said Superintendent Lahan, standing at the podium in a flowing black commencement gown, "able to converse in at least two languages, a contributing force in the life of the school, with the ability to bring differing people together into a sense of community."

I could see my father, leaning over and translating to Jiddo Riyad, my mother doing the same for Taytay.

"This year's Award for International Understanding goes to Luma Mufleh."

As I stood to receive my award, the crowd stood as well. My mother, father, grandfather, and Taytay clapping the loudest of them all. Even Jiddo Riyad was smiling. Aunt Abla gave me a thumbs-up. A merciful moment of joy.

After the ceremony, I joined my family in the back of the auditorium.

"I have the tablas waiting outside!" Abla said, referring to the noisy drums Arabs play in celebration. She was always threatening to show my Western friends just how Arab my family really was. I was just relieved she didn't wear her gorilla mask.

My grandmother was the first to wrap me in her arms. She whispered, "You are so much like our side of the family."

Luckily, my grandfather didn't hear. Instead of a hug, he gave me a curt nod. "You made the Muflehs proud today," he told me.

"Yalla!" Abla roused us all to get moving, back to the party at our house.

I couldn't help but feel cheered up by the festivities, all the friends and family in one room for me. So I didn't get into Brown, but New York was still in America, still a place where I might find a way to live life fully on my terms, whatever that looked like. I wasn't even jealous when a group of partygoers began making plans for an afterparty at a club. Besides, the thought of going to the club with kids I hardly knew—pretending I wanted to dance with boys and not girls or pretending the boy I was dancing with *was* a girl—did not appeal to me. A half dozen of my friends were sleeping over anyway; my party would still continue well into the night.

My cousin Subhi was among those heading to the club. He had flown in earlier that week from the US, where he was studying at Vanderbilt. "Come on, I'll ask Ammo," he said, offering to ask my parents to let me join.

"It's okay, Subhi, it's not that big a deal."

"You know they'll say yes if I ask," Subhi said with the same toothy grin he had had since we were kids. I knew he was right. The youngest of six and the only boy, Subhi was beloved. He got what he wanted.

"No, no, it's been a great day, and I just want to hang out with the girls."

"Okay," he said, putting his blazer back on. "I'll see you later in the week at Jiddo's lunch."

Hours later, in the steely black of early morning, I woke up to the phone ringing and the hall light coming on. We were sprawled out on blankets and mattresses across the floor.

The phone rang again.

There was a gasp and then the slam of the front door. I heard my mother's feet on the stairs.

She stood in the doorway for a moment, trying to figure out which shapeless form was mine. I didn't want her to find me, didn't want to know whatever she had come to tell me.

"Luma, come with me," she said, her fingers on my shoulder.

"It's too early," I whispered.

"Come with me," she repeated, not angry.

"Why?"

"Subhi was in a car accident. He's dead."

CHAPTER 13
FUGITIVE

THE PARK WASN'T a very pretty park, and so it was usually empty. A couple acres a few miles outside of the city, it was a simple place: a smattering of picnic tables beneath pine trees that somehow grew from sand and rock. In the summer, it was miserably hot, and Susan and I could count on being the only ones there.

Susan was on top of me, her brown hair a curtain around our faces. I had my hands on her hips; hers were on my shoulders. It was stupid, so risky. But in the week following Subhi's death, I couldn't stop thinking that I should have been in his car. That I should have been the dead one. Maybe that's why I called Susan.

Maybe there was a breeze or birdsong or the sound of footsteps, but I heard nothing until the unmistakable crackle of a walkie-talkie filled the silence. I felt Susan's weight slide from my torso, and then the sun was in my eyes.

"Koomi," a man said in Arabic. I shifted my head toward the voice to see the small barrel of a handgun. The police officer holding it was in plain clothes, but his shiny black dress shoes gave him away. His face was red and sweaty; he looked to be the same age as Uncle Khaled, maybe thirty.

"Get up," I translated to Susan, who whimpered but complied.

"What do you want from us?" she pleaded, her arms raised toward the sky, tears pooling beneath her eyes.

I shook my head. "Just listen to him."

The officer used his gun to motion us toward the parking lot. "Imshi."

"Move it," I told Susan. As we walked to my car, each step felt heavier than the last. If I refused to move, I thought, maybe he would just shoot me now and get it over with.

After seconds that felt like hours, the hot metal of the door handle was in my hand. I slid into the driver's seat, where my right foot fell instinctually on the gas pedal. Susan appeared in the passenger seat, now visibly shaking. The back door opened; the officer lumbered into the seat behind me. In the rearview mirror, I watched him place the gun on the leather upholstery beside his leg.

"What were you doing?" he demanded.

I cleared my throat before I realized that there was no answer. If I lied, he would know. If I told the truth, he would kill me.

"Do you know what you were doing?" he repeated, this time louder.

I cleared my throat again, sputtering like a broken engine.

"What do you want from us?" Susan screeched. I winced at the desperation and fear in her voice. She sounded like a terrified child. Susan didn't realize that as an American, she was hardly in danger. If something happened to her, the embassy would get involved—Jordan didn't want a diplomatic scandal on their hands. The consequences would be worse for me, the Arab.

"One of you speaks Arabic," came the voice from the back seat, growing more impatient.

Why had I been so reckless? In two months, I would sit between my parents on a plane bound for New York City. In two months, I would be free. But instead of lying low and being safe, I had driven this woman here, to this park, to make out where anyone could find us. Maybe part of me wanted to get caught; maybe that death wish had never really gone away.

"Are you a virgin?"

My pulse loud in my ears, my throat twisted like a wrung-out sponge, I tried to speak. I could not.

"I can take you down to the station right now and find out." I thought about Khalo's wedding, the bloody sheet emerging from a dark room. I knew the officer wasn't bluffing.

"Adish bidak?" Susan's head jerked toward me, surprised as I was to hear myself speak. *How much do you want?*

"Get out," he said to Susan in forced English. I heard Susan inhale sharply, and then she did as she was told.

"You want money." My mind and mouth were operating fully in Arabic now, a language that has no patience for weakness.

"What's your name?" he said. The words tightened my stomach.

"Forty? Sixty?" I had seen my cousins bribe countless police officers to get out of speeding tickets.

"I can run the license plate."

"One hundred?"

"Give me your license. Now."

This was it. He would see my name, he would call my family, and I would be killed. I had brought dishonor. I pulled my wallet from my back pocket. Without turning around, I held my ID above my right shoulder. I pictured the words as the officer read them: *Luma Hassan Riyad Mufleh.* My father and grandfather might as well have been sitting in the car next to me. The silence went on forever.

Finally, he spoke. "I saw nothing."

Now there was fear in his voice. There was some movement, and then his shoulders squeezed through the seats, his fingers tightened around my forearm.

"Your cousin. I am so sorry for your family's loss." His words were rushed and frightened, the opposite of before. He flipped my arm over. "Are you on drugs?" he asked, as he looked for evidence on the inside of my elbow. "Is this why?"

I shook my head.

"Show me your other arm." I twisted in my seat to comply. "Don't let them do this to you," he said as he inspected my skin. Still holding my arm, he shook me slightly. "Don't ever see her again."

I nodded.

He put my ID on the armrest and got out of the car. Through the sealed windows I heard him apologize to Susan. "No more," he attempted to say in English. Seconds later, Susan was in the seat next to me, her breathing fast and erratic. It felt impossible that ten minutes ago I had been kissing this woman. Now I was repulsed by her fragility, resentful that I was the one who needed to reassure her.

I never saw her again, but not because the officer had forbidden it.

FOR DAYS, I waited. For the phone call, for the knock on the door. The officer would tell the others, I knew it. Word would eventually get to my uncle Ayman, a member of the Mukhabarat, Jordan's infamous intelligence agency. It was summer, so it was easy enough to stay home, to be the first to jump up when the phone rang. To lie around reading as if I wasn't nauseous with dread.

It seemed miraculous then, to land in Limassol, Cyprus,

for our last summer vacation less than a week later. I still felt like an escaped convict, still jumped when the maid knocked on the hotel door. Every man I saw was that police officer, walking toward me with his gun, screaming my name. I would imagine him shooting me point-blank, or worse, announcing to everyone what he had seen me do. No one else on the trip seemed like they were having much fun either; the shock of Subhi's death had given way to a heavy sadness that seemed to make everyone move slowly, speak quietly.

Still, Cyprus felt safer than Jordan. Ali, Saeed, and I took a certification course in scuba diving. When we learned that flying less than twenty-four hours after a dive could result in serious illness, all I heard was how to avoid going home. On the last afternoon of our trip, I scheduled our longest, deepest dive yet, and played dumb when we returned to our parents at the hotel to tell them they would have to push our flights back another day.

With those final hours of refuge, I sat on the beach and stared at the waves, mesmerized by the swell and crash of each one. I thought about how life had felt a lot like that lately—huge surges of hope—Julie, my parents' pride at graduation—followed by devastating blows. The letter from Brown, the gun in my hand, Subhi, the gun at my head.

I felt so much shame, not for who I was but for what I had done. The relationship with Susan had been a terrible mistake. She had taken advantage of me, used my vulnerability to get what she wanted. But when push came to shove, during those long minutes in the car, Susan didn't care what happened to me. Had my last name not been Mufleh, I would have been raped or killed, and Susan would have watched it happen. I had felt so inflated that out of everyone, Susan had chosen me. But of course she had chosen me. Who else would have been so willing to hide everything? To not say a word to anyone? Thinking back on all the hours we spent together, I could hardly recognize myself in those memories.

I could see that ever since that night with the pills, I *had* become two versions of myself, two Lumas.

One Luma listened to her heart, to the voice that told me my place was in Jordan, picking fruit with my grandmother, pulling pranks on younger cousins with Abla, playing soccer with my friends. That Luma was determined to believe there was a way forward, that family and enough prayer could fix anything.

The other Luma believed her head, what it had always known to be true. There was no future in Jordan, no way to make the puzzle pieces fit. That Luma had tried over and over to wake the other one up, pointing out the inequalities of Jordanian society, the inconsistencies of Islam. That Luma had also been rash and reckless, ready to confront death head-on instead of waiting for it to sneak up behind her.

I hated that police officer, but I also owed him a debt.

He'd showed me the impossibility of living two lives. These two parts of me could not coexist; I had to decide once and for all who I was going to be.

I lay back on the sand and stared up at the purple sky. What would my life look like in America? I let my mind wander back into one of my favorite daydreams. In it, I was dating one of the girls in *The Cosby Show*. I imagined myself walking up the stairs to their brownstone, knocking on those black double doors. Mrs. Huxtable greeted me with a familiar smile and led me into the kitchen, where we all, the Huxtable girls and me, sat around the table and talked about our days.

Another wave crashed, and I couldn't help but smile at the idea.

CHAPTER 14
TAKEOFF

THE NIGHT BEFORE I left for America, there was a big family get-together held in my honor at Jiddo Riyad's. I kept my gaze fixed between the clock and the door, waiting for the night to end or for the police officer to barge in. But nothing happened; we ate hummus, foul, taboulleh, falafel kaak, and eggs. We said our goodbyes. We drove home in silence through the thick summer heat.

The next day, I wandered around the house like a lost dog, waiting for my parents to finish packing. They had started calling this trip their "college-moon." My mother had been telling me for weeks that she couldn't wait to land in New York City.

"You're going to love it," she had told me.

"Do you think it'll be the same as it was when you were there? I mean, now they have cars and—"

"Oh, be quiet. It's the feeling, the feeling will be the same."

Finally, the suitcases were stacked in the back of the Range Rover, my brothers, sister, and I settled in the back seat. I studied my brothers' profiles and wondered which one would get the code to the safe now that I was gone.

Five minutes later, we arrived at my grandmother's house. Taytay and Abla were waiting outside as we pulled up to say goodbye. I had spent virtually all of my time with Taytay in those last few weeks, cooking and devouring all the dishes I loved like it was the last time I would ever eat them.

Ali and Saeed jumped out of the car and disappeared into the house, where they would be staying while we were in America. I helped Inam from the car, held her chubby seven-year-old hand as she marched up the front steps. When she saw Sara and Leila, Abla's daughters, she tore her fingers from mine and ran over to play. So much for missing me.

"I can't believe you are going to college—do they know you are really not that smart?" Abla teased, wrapping an arm around my shoulder. "It's going to be so fun."

"And work. Lots of work."

Abla frowned at me. "It's going to be *fun*. Stop focusing on the studying."

I looked to see if my father was listening. If he thought for one second I was going to America to have fun, he'd never let me go.

"She knows that if she fails any of her classes, she'll be on the first plane home," he said with a half smile.

"She won't fail a class," my mother boasted. "She's never even failed a test."

One last time, Taytay folded me up in her arms. Her dress smelled like the garden, like tomatoes and parsley and afternoon sun. "Habibti," she whispered.

As I walked to the car, my parents lingered near my grandmother.

"That one's not coming back," I heard her say. A panic rose in my chest.

"Of course she is—she'll be back in December," my father said, no hint of worry in his voice.

Once we were on the highway, I put my head against the cool glass of the window and watched the desert race by, a blur of browns and reds. My mother turned around to look at me.

"Inam will miss you."

"She won't even realize I'm gone. And she already gave me a list of all the toys she wants."

"Are you sad?" she asked, squeezing my knee.

"No, not at all." It was the biggest lie I had told yet.

PART II

CHAPTER 15
LANDING

"IF YOU LOOK to your left, ladies and gentlemen, you'll see the Statue of Liberty."

Heeding the pilot's words, I craned my neck and narrowed my eyes, trying to look past the reflected glare of the cabin to see the gigantic statue in the water. Behind her, New York City's skyline sparkled.

Big cities were not new to me. I had been to London and Cairo and Hong Kong. But compared to New York, those places now seemed flat and homogenous; the same faces, the same voices, the same smells permeated the streets. In New York, every block was an orchestra of languages: Arabic, Korean, French, Spanish, Japanese, and the distinct New York accent. Everyone sounded like they were in *Seinfeld*. The mouthwatering smells of kebabs, pizza, fried rice, and tacos had me figuring out how I could try all of them at once, and save room for all the other delicious scents I couldn't quite place. More than anything, though, it was the spirit that energized me, the pulsing buzz of humanity on display around every corner—everyone moved like they were on the way to the most important moment of their life.

Most of the memories I have of those first days in America are blurry at best, but some encounters stand out to me even now. Buying a hot dog from the first hot dog stand I saw (shawarma who?), realizing the cabdrivers were just as wild as the ones back home (*Close your eyes and pray*, we used to say), and sitting on the top of a double-decker bus, getting sunburnt while the tour guide's animated voice crackled through the headphones.

We drove through Chinatown, through Times Square and Greenwich Village, where the bus idled in front of the Stonewall Inn. This, the tour guide reported, was where gay people fought back against yet another police raid, igniting weeks of protests and kick-starting a movement that demanded the end of persecution based on sexual orientation. I tried to visualize these protests, curious if they were anything like the ones I had seen at home protesting the rising cost of bread or the lack of employment opportunities. Had the police used tear gas or wielded sticks to beat up the protestors? Or were the drag queens fighting back with their high heels and purses? Protests in Jordan were snuffed out swiftly, but in America, apparently dissent could get things done. The tour guide continued, saying that in large cities across America, annual gay pride parades celebrated the June anniversary of what became known as the Stonewall Uprising. I didn't know if I should feel relieved or disappointed that I had missed the celebrations by a few months.

The story quickened my breath; as subtly as I could, I inspected my parents' faces, the faces of the other tourgoers, for their reactions. But there was nothing there, just a matter-of-factness that both comforted and confused me. In fact, ever since we had landed in New York they had seemed different, more laid-back and affectionate with each other.

After three days in the city, we flew to Syracuse, where everything was a vibrant shade of green. My father drove us to Geneva, where I would go through a week of orientation at Hobart and William Smith while they would enjoy sleeping late in a nearby vacation cottage that overlooked a tranquil blue lake.

I had connected with my roommate through letters while I was still in Amman. Vanessa was from a suburb of New York City, but her parents were originally from Belgium. She had a barely detectable French accent. She ended up being one of my only friends at HWS that didn't graduate from a New England prep school. In some ways, even though I was an international student, I fit in more than Vanessa. I didn't *want* to be on the ski or sailing team, but I had been on skis, on a sailboat. And like most of my classmates, I didn't have to worry about paying for books or nights out.

During orientation, I joined the small contingent of international students in a meeting to fill out all the necessary government documentation to legally reside in the United States during the next four years. I zipped through the first few questions easily: name, birthday, address. Next up was citizenship; I glanced through the options but had trouble discerning their meaning. I was relieved when another student asked which one we should select.

"Legal alien authorized to work in the US," one of the advisors recited.

An alien? I pictured E.T. as I reluctantly checked the box.

The next question was even more confounding. Race, it turned out, wasn't just an athletic event. As I scoured the choices, it dawned on me that "race" was the American version of "tribe." But which one did I belong to?

American Indian? No.

Black/African American? No.

Hawaiian/Pacific Islander? No.

Hispanic or Latino? No.

Asian? I guess? Technically? Though I had never thought of myself like that. I thought of myself as Jordanian. As a Mufleh. To me, Americans were Americans.

White? I held my hand at eye level. It *was* kind of white, but also a little tan from the sun. I flipped it around. Pink.

I furtively looked around the room to find the student from Saudi Arabia. Was he going to check *Asian*? I wondered. Weren't we both *Arab*?

The dean must have seen one Middle Eastern student looking at another and figured out what was happening.

"If you're from the Middle East, you will choose white," he said.

At this, the Saudi kid snapped to attention. "I'm not white, I'm brown," he said, and he was, much darker than me. "Aren't I Asian?"

"You are not Asian, you are white."

Apparently, whatever government agency created this form didn't realize there were tens of millions of people living in the Middle East and northern Africa. Surely we were worthy of our own box, I thought. They could have at least given us *other*. It seemed unfair that some got to check off exactly who they were, while others weren't even listed on the form.

I did as I was told and checked *white*. I stared at the checkmark for a few seconds trying to think of myself as white. Then I checked the *Asian* box, too.

At first, I figured that only the government and school administrators cared about these kinds of demographics, but then I saw my classmates self-segregating around the same fault lines. As I walked around the activities fair, where all the clubs and student groups on campus gathered to recruit new members, I couldn't help but notice similar divisions. There were clubs for international students, Black students, and Latin American students. There was one for Jews, one for Christians, another for Muslims. There was even a club for gay and lesbian students (at the time known as LGB students).

I didn't quite understand how this was supposed to work. What about a Black Muslim student—what group would they join, both? What kind of Islam did the Muslim group practice? Did you have to pray? I didn't pray. Would that disqualify me? Did picking the international club mean I was choosing that part of me over the gay part? I found myself hovering on the edges, reluctant to get sucked into any one persuasion. This was not the moment to be labeled or stuck in a category, and I was warily protective of the freedom I had waited so long for.

On the night before they left for Jordan, my parents asked me to bring some of my suitemates to their rented lake house, where they would cook a Middle Eastern feast for us. My mother gave me a list, and my new friends and I headed to the grocery store. There, I stood transfixed in front of the wall of olive oils: virgin, extra virgin, premium, pure. If I had arrived in the United States thinking I understood one thing, it was olive oil. But it wasn't just oil, every aisle overflowed with choice: Coke *or* Pepsi, Heinz *or* Hunt's, Kraft *or* Velveeta.

In their provisional kitchen, my parents worked culinary miracles, wowing these American girls by serving chicken and rice stew, kebabs, and taboulleh. Later, when I realized that I had moved to a town that didn't contain a bite of authentic Middle Eastern food, I would curse myself for not savoring that dinner more. (And I would call my grandmother, begging for a recipe, only to be reminded that she didn't have any, just lists of ingredients and her nose.)

Those are the last snapshots in my mind of my parents in Geneva during the fall of 1993. I hardly remember saying goodbye to them; it was as if the novelty of everything, of all the things I wanted to do and see, had hijacked my senses, temporarily turning off my ability to feel sad.

I do remember the first thing I did after they left, though. I got a haircut. Under the fluorescent glow of a discount salon, I let the stylist chop off most of my sun-drenched curls while I studied the pleasing way they gathered in half-moons on the vinyl floor.

KEVIN'S HAIR WAS longer than mine, silky and straight and down to his shoulders. He was tall with a wiry frame, and the Banana Republic clothes he wore made him look like a model. The first time I saw him was at the student activities fair, where he was manning the LGB table. A few days later, Kevin didn't so much introduce himself as appear beside me in the cafeteria and start talking. Right away, I could tell that he was incredibly smart and delightfully sarcastic.

"So are you going to join the group?" he asked.

"Wait, how did you know that I'm—"

"Gay?"

"Yeah. Gay."

"Gaydar."

"Gaydar?"

Kevin rolled his eyes playfully. "You know your people," he clarified.

Kevin and his friend Steve became my people. (Maybe "frenemy" is the better term for what they were to each other. Though they hung out together, there was a lot of tension between Kevin and Steve. Kevin was smarter; Steve liked to party. Steve came from money; Kevin didn't. But they were two of only a handful of out men, so they stuck together or were stuck together; it didn't really matter which.) They took me to my first gay bar, a place in Ithaca, a larger college town about an hour away. There, I watched in wonder as same-sex couples crowded the dance floor, their hands floating and faces touching, a happy mass of bodies. My suitemates—all straight women—had come with us. For those few hours, it felt possible that being gay didn't have to feel secret and shameful, that in fact it could be a part of my life other people could appreciate and enjoy. On the drive home, Vanessa even complained that no one hit on her.

"Am I not cute enough?" she asked. "Not a good enough dancer?"

"You're not gay enough," Steve said from the driver's seat.

"How do they know?"

"Gaydar!" Kevin and I said in unison.

Kevin and Steve weren't too impressed with Ithaca's nightlife and soon planned a trip for us to New York City. On a Saturday in late November, we made our pilgrimage, kicking off the day with a cocktail at the Stonewall Inn, where the counter was sticky and the whole place sagged in disrepair. I felt disappointed that this landmark hadn't been more lovingly preserved, but it was a bar, after all.

If Stonewall was a bit of a letdown, the dance clubs and drag shows we went to more than made up for it. They vaguely reminded me of the few nightclubs I had been allowed to visit with my cousins on vacations in London and Athens, but were a million times better since I wouldn't have to worry about being hit on—at least not by men. When I approached the bartender to get another bottle of water, a woman, who appeared to be at least fifteen years older, with a marine-like buzz cut, a white T-shirt, leather jacket, and jeans, smiled and nodded at me. I smiled and nodded back. But she wasn't hitting on me; that was a different look. She, like the other men and women in the bar, seemed to be telling me, *I am like you, I know what you have been through, and it's going to be okay.*

The bars were dizzyingly loud and euphoric, the energy inside so palpable the air felt heavy with it. For so long I had thought I was the only one with these feelings; how strange and liberating it was to be in rooms full of people just like me. How strange and liberating it felt to no longer have to pretend or create imaginary worlds. I could dance and smile and flirt with any girl in the bar, didn't have to imagine the boy I was dancing with in a skirt or makeup to make him more feminine. I didn't have to be guarded and watch my back to see if anyone noticed I was an imposter. As "Tina Trainer" took the stage, I watched the audience clap and cheer, mouths wide open not in disgust but in awe of the majestic performance. No one laughed or snickered or judged here; we all were celebrating and accepting every different part of what made us whole. The dance floor shook in unison as we all belted out, "What's love got to do with it?" Knowing full well it had everything to do with it.

Maybe freedom is hard to value if you've never gone without it. My suitemates couldn't fully appreciate the magic of the gay bar, and my classmates didn't seem half as enamored of the privilege that our classes provided us—a space to ask questions and voice our opinions without fear. My British and American schools had encouraged free thinking—to a point. We, teachers and students, knew better than to criticize the Jordanian government, for example, or to discuss the social issues that were pervasive in our country and region. Open political discourse, even more than the nightlife, was the best part of America.

I purposely took classes that challenged the version of the world I had learned about in Jordan. Outside of school, I had been taught that the blue stripes on the Israeli flag, for instance, represented the Nile and the Euphrates, and the white space represented all of the land in between, land the Jews would take for their own if given the opportunity. My uncles said that all Jews and Israelis were aligned with the Zionist agenda and their goal was to eradicate our country and occupy our lands. In school, my textbooks didn't even show Israel on the map. Now, in my freshman college courses, I was exposed to the Holocaust, to Anne Frank and Elie Wiesel.

One class in particular tested me, the History and Politics of Israel and Zionism. I was the only non-Jewish student in the class. My frustration and anger grew after continuously hearing justifications for the violence against Palestinians. Would they justify the car bomb that was placed in my friend's father's car that left him with both legs amputated after the assassination attempt? Could they look past the thousands languishing in the refugee camp Taytay had taken me to? I didn't want to know the answer. After class I approached my professor, requesting that she sign the withdrawal form.

"Why?" she asked.

"It's just not my thing."

"But aren't you from Jordan?"

"Yes, so this stuff is, you know, boring." I shrugged.

"Boring?"

"I mean, it conflicts with my schedule."

"Mm-hm."

I was realizing she wasn't going to sign the form if I didn't tell the truth.

"It's all the same thing. 'Israel is great,' 'Israel does no harm.'"

"And that's why I am not signing the form."

"What? Being in this class is not going to change—"

"Others, including me, need to hear what you have to say. If there is no other perspective, how will we learn? How will we learn if we are never challenged?"

"But it's not my responsibility."

"Yes, it is. I am not signing," she said. And she didn't. The class didn't end up changing my perspective, but it made me more aware of nuances and other sides to a story. I became acutely aware of how two people can view a singular event very differently—different heroes, different villains.

I was, however, successful in withdrawing from the women's studies class. Long discussions on issues like pornography, prostitution, and breastfeeding in public felt small and unimportant given what challenges women in my own country faced.

I did not want to discuss the pros and cons of pornography. I wanted to discuss honor killings, women as property, and what could be done to change that. Who cared if you wanted to be a prostitute and were worried about how your parents were going to react? I cared about bloody sheets, gouged eyeballs, and smashed skulls.

I also learned that the region I had grown up in—what for me had always been the center of the world—was hardly a blip on most Americans' radars. I got good at the geography lesson I inevitably had to give when people asked where I was from. ("It's a small country in the Middle East, sandwiched between Iraq and Israel/Palestine.") And it quickly became apparent that if my classmates thought about the Middle East at all, their impressions had been shaped by either the Gulf War or some movie like *Lawrence of Arabia*.

During a conversation after class, a doughy frat boy with blue eyes peppered me with questions about my upbringing in this exotic land. "So, did you, like, ride a camel to school?" he asked.

I was quiet for a moment. I couldn't tell if he was serious or mocking. I knew that I should be generous, take the opportunity to dispel the antiquated ideas Westerners had about my culture, but I couldn't resist the fun.

"Yes, sure did," I said, with as much sincerity as I could muster.

"You did?" he gasped, his eyebrows sliding up his forehead.

"Actually, I rode a two-humped camel," I said, leaning in like I was about to share a secret, "which is what you want if you can afford it. With the two humps, it's more comfortable—you can relax and don't have to hold on too tight."

Other fibs I told about the Middle East weren't as playful, like when Vanessa asked about how gay people were treated in Jordan.

"It doesn't go over well," I answered, hardly looking up from the desk in our room, where I was studying. Thankfully, Vanessa didn't question this brazen understatement, sparing me from having to talk about—or dwell on—my still-uncertain future.

Though the bright spots remained, the honeymoon phase at HWS didn't last, and there were lots of moments like this, like I was a square peg trying to jam myself into a round hole. The campus and surrounding town could feel claustrophobic and conservative. One of the school's gay professors was attacked on National Coming Out Day; he walked into class the next day with two black eyes. My teammates on the freshman soccer team seemed to play the sport in a mechanical, joyless way that hardly resembled the game I so loved. And then there were the academics, which didn't feel particularly challenging.

I had walked into my first-year classes thinking I would be way behind. Surely these American kids who had attended some of the most expensive schools in the world would be leaps and bounds ahead of me. This assumption motivated me to work three times as hard as everyone else, to stay up until all hours of the night copying my lecture notes and endlessly editing my papers. My single-mindedness paid off in the form of straight A's and high praise from my teachers. Once, I sat low in my seat, blushing as my writing professor wondered aloud to the class how the Jordanian student had managed to write a better English paper than kids who grew up *only* speaking English.

It was that same writing professor who encouraged me to consider transferring. I wouldn't have thought much of it, but then my advisor also suggested I look at other schools. Both of them urged me to think about a women's college, where I might be more challenged academically and fulfilled personally. They assured me that women's colleges weren't glorified finishing schools but first-class institutions. That there, I would find the diversity I obviously craved—of ideas, of international students, of women who cared about the things I did. There, they told me, I would not be the smartest student in the room.

It was a few weeks before winter break when I made up my mind to transfer, right around the time that the nightmares began.

CHAPTER 16
SWITCHING

MY STOMACH HURT. Nothing I ate would stay down. As the winter grew colder and grayer, I began waking up trembling and drenched in sweat. One morning, Vanessa told me I had been screaming in my sleep. I acted surprised, saying I couldn't remember my nightmare, but that wasn't true. I had dreamt of the police officer, of his dark silhouette and his gleaming pistol, waiting for me in the terminal of the Amman airport.

The date I would travel home had been set months in advance. My father had booked me on a round trip when we came to America, and the ticket to Jordan had sat in my top desk drawer all semester. There was no getting around it; I had to go. I tried to focus on the positives: seeing my sister, eating Taytay's cooking. I filled my time with practice exams and writing essays; I stayed up all night to avoid the nightmares.

The switch, as I began to think of it, happened somewhere over the Atlantic Ocean. I would feel it again on every return flight. It was an almost physical sensation, like the swinging of a gauge, when *what I cannot do* transformed into *what I must do*, when resistance hardened into resignation.

As the plane taxied in Amman, I lifted the window shade to greet the desert's furious sunlight. After my first taste of winter, it was not a wholly unwelcome sight. My heart was buoyed by my mother's arms, the familiar smell of the Range Rover, highways I knew by heart. In fact, thousands of miles away from the classrooms and nightclubs of New York, it was easier than I had thought to fall back into my old role as big sister and dutiful daughter and doting granddaughter. After all, I had been those things much longer than the American version of me.

I came bearing gifts—Legos and books for Inam and handfuls of Dubble Bubble for Abla. I assured my mom that my dark hair wasn't dyed but sun-deprived. (She didn't like the short cut, but my biggest sin was losing its Syrian lightness.) I inhaled plates of Taytay's meals, which she had methodically planned to make sure I got all my favorites. Mostly, I spent two weeks lying low, avoiding situations that might attract any attention—being a woman driving late at night, for instance, or being a Muslim with a drink in my hand at a club with my cousins. I stayed in the spaces I knew were safe, the spaces where the police officer wouldn't be. And I began plotting my campaign for transferring schools.

I knew just how to start. "You were right," I told my father, who I found reading in the living room one night after dinner. At those three words, he looked up, already wearing a victorious smile.

"About what?"

"My advisor—and that writing professor I told you about—they think I should transfer to a women's college. I think I should, too."

My father closed his book and set it beside him.

"Smith College in Massachusetts," he said, "produced both Nancy Reagan and Barbara Bush."

"That would be nice, habibti," my mother chimed in. "Then we could just fly into Boston. No long drives to New York."

"You could also look at Wellesley," my father offered. I nodded obediently, confident that the conversation had already swung my way. By the time my flight left Amman in early January, my father had helped me schedule tours at both Smith and Wellesley.

The spring semester had barely started when I flew east to check out Smith College. After all but a few hours in Northampton, Massachusetts, my mind was made up. Unlike my classes at HWS, where the men mostly dominated the conversation, in the classes I sat in on at Smith, every single woman participated in lively, sometimes heated, discussions, each one declaring something smarter than the last. Around campus, I saw so many gay couples holding hands I lost count. In the city's bustling downtown, I didn't feel the buzz of New York City, admittedly, but a buzz all the same. It felt like a place with an open mind and a big heart and an authentic personality. There was a Thai restaurant, a sushi joint, and even a hole-in-the-wall that sold falafel and tabouleh, terrible by my grandmother's standards but significant for its mere existence. When I got back to Geneva, I canceled my tour of Wellesley.

The next three months passed quickly. Before I was ready (would I ever really be ready?), it was time for goodbyes—to Vanessa, Kevin, Steve, and the spring-green hills of New York. And it was time for the nightmares, the sweaty mornings, and the transatlantic switch all over again.

HWS WAS ON a trimester system, Smith on semesters. Because I would need to take summer courses to meet entrance requirements at Smith, I was able to whittle my break in Jordan down to a matter of weeks. On my second trip back, I felt a little more confident, more comfortable spending time with friends in a few select, safe places. One of those was my old high school, where I attended graduation to cheer on my younger friends as they walked across the stage.

That night after the ceremony, I invited a few of them over to our house instead of wherever the afterparty was being held. After the rest of them had left, Yaseen, my would-be prom date, and our friend Maya remained, sitting on the floor of my room in front of the CD player. They were catching me up on the gossip, the makeups and breakups, and telling stories about past romantic dramas. All night Yaseen had been barraging me with questions about Massachusetts because in a few months he was moving there, too, to attend Hampshire College, a fifteen-minute drive from Smith.

"When I asked you out last year, why didn't you say yes?" Yaseen asked, laughing nervously.

"Don't be ridiculous. I wasn't going to date you."

"Why not?" Yaseen pretended to be hurt.

"The better question is why did you ask? You're not attracted to me."

"I just wanted to be able to say I had dated Luma Mufleh, to be the only one that could say that."

"That's a stupid reason to date someone," I said, giving Yaseen a sisterly punch in the shoulder. Maya giggled.

"So you're not attracted to *me*?"

"You're not my type." I waited, wondering if Yaseen wanted me to be the first to say it. Maybe a year ago, I wouldn't have, but now I could feel that something inside of me had changed, that some of the old shame was gone. I thought of the look that woman in the leather jacket had given me in the bar, the way her simple nod made me feel seen and accepted. Could I be that person for Yaseen now? "I'm attracted to people like Maya, just like you're attracted to people like Amin."

At first, Yaseen pretended to be disgusted. "Gross!" he said.

"I'm attracted to people like Maya. You're attracted to people like Amin," I repeated.

Yaseen's shoulders softened. He looked down at the carpet and released a long sigh. When he looked back up, his eyes were worried.

"How did you know?"

"Gaydar," I announced, and then closed my door so I could tell him all about the drag queens in New York City.

CHAPTER 17
A NEW HOUSE

LATER, WE WOULD laugh about it. Our misguided stereotypes. Seeing my name and where I was from on her roster of new residents, Dee-Ann expected a demure woman wearing a hijab. When I walked up the front stairs of my new dorm and saw Dee-Ann, her red hair chopped as short as mine, I assumed she was gay.

"I'm Luma," I said.

"*You're* Luma?" she said with a wide smile, looking down at her clipboard. "I'm Dee-Ann. I'm the head resident."

I nodded, shifting my duffel bag from one shoulder to the other. Dee-Ann asked how she could help me get settled in. Her blue eyes were clear and friendly.

"Just my room number," I said.

"Oh, right! You're in thirty-five. We have a house meeting tonight I hope you'll come to. We'll all introduce ourselves, get to know each other, and just go over house rules and stuff like that."

"Of course, I'll be there."

Unlike the majority of students, who were being dropped off by their parents, I arrived alone, having spent the previous week at another international student orientation. I was relieved to be without my mom and dad as I watched my peers negotiate this rite of passage with theirs. Parents wanting to make sure that their daughters had every last thing they needed. Daughters who wanted to be independent. Others trying to prolong the goodbye as much as possible. Instead of that hassle, I threw my bag and my bedding into my room and came back downstairs to help the other new students move in.

As I introduced myself and carried mini fridges and bulletin boards up the stairs, I felt a lightness, a sense of being *at home*. Maybe it was only being around women, or maybe it was because our residence was an actual house. All the dorms on Smith's campus were houses; there were forty-one of them. Mine was called Capen. It was a beautiful white mansion with four Ionic columns that soared above a massive front porch. During my tour of Smith, I had been told that the sixty or so residents of my house and I would eat meals together, watch movies together, and work on community service projects together. On Friday afternoons, we would take a break from everything—classes, clubs, sports— to have tea together. Inside, we would exist as a familial unit; outside, the campus was idyllic and peaceful.

That evening at the house meeting, as I looked around

at the women gathered in a large circle, I noticed how different we all were. I knew there would be students from each year in my house, but I hadn't realized just how diverse it would be. There were women in dresses and makeup, and women in Doc Martens and leather jackets. There were different ethnicities and racial identities. No one looked the same, no one dressed the same, but from that moment on, we would share a common identity—we were Smithies.

Dee-Ann began the introductions by telling us about herself. She was a senior, she said, originally from Ohio and an English major. Sheherazade was a sophomore from Connecticut who had written to me over the summer to welcome me to Smith. (My dad had been excited for me to befriend Sheherazade, whom he correctly identified as a Muslim. Her mom was Irish, but he would have been dismayed to know that her dad was a non-practicing Muslim.) Misty was a curvy yellow-haired girl from Maine, an anthropology major. (I would declare anthropology my major soon after. For an introvert who likes to learn about other cultures, about other ways of being in the world, it was the perfect spot for me.)

After introductions snaked their way around the room, residents began breaking off into smaller groups, chatting with the people around them. I found myself in conversation with a few women, asking about hometowns, their siblings. Someone asked what my parents did for a living.

I thought for a moment, not wanting to reveal too much. "My dad is in steel," I said slowly, satisfied that my answer was technically truthful.

"What about your mom?" someone else asked.

"My mom sleeps with my dad." This got some laughs, including, I noticed, from Misty. I decided right away that I liked her.

Later that night, I stepped into Misty's open door and tapped on it. Nearly everything inside was pink. Pink curtains, pink comforter, pink pillows. I had always hated the color pink, maybe because it was foisted on me, but in Misty's charge, the ultrafeminine was somehow cozy; it matched her rosy cheeks and porcelain skin. She looked like an eighteenth-century milkmaid. But I quickly learned that Misty's sweet exterior was a cover for her wild and irreverent personality. Over the next few months and then years, Misty and I would rarely be apart.

All the women of Capen were fast friends, though. We piled into someone's car for trips to the grocery store or the mall and sang along to old songs like "Oh, What a Night" and "Come On, Eileen." We stormed the dance floor any time "I Will Survive" by Gloria Gaynor came on; it became our anthem. We walked to downtown coffee shops arm in arm, taking up the entire sidewalk. We spent long hours and all-nighters in each other's rooms; we peed with the door open to not interrupt the conversation. We went to classes together, to parties together, and (too often) to the World War II Club together, a Northampton dive bar where Smithies mixed with chain-smoking townies. A place where no one batted an eye at a baby-faced blonde slamming a Jäger shot, or a Muslim nursing a vodka cranberry, or the two of them belting out "Little Red Corvette" at karaoke night.

I WAS COLLECTING contradictions like a bouquet of flowers. It was hard to hold them all at once. I never ate pork, but I drank vodka. I never prayed, but I fasted all of Ramadan. I believed, just as my religion had told me, that there was only one God and that Muhammad (PBUH) was his messenger— yet I slept with women.

I also started feeling more confident in fighting for others who had struggled like me. I joined the LGB club and began attending protests in Massachusetts and Washington, DC, writing speeches for those who would speak there. I marched in support of funding for AIDS; I spoke out about the violence in the Middle East, advocating for peaceful solutions. I wrote op-eds in the campus newspaper, though always under a pseudonym. This behind-the-scenes work suited my introverted personality; the freedom to speak out was intoxicating.

In a way, I felt the same level of delirium when dating

women. I was like a kid in a candy store, I fell in love with the first thing I saw and fell out just as quick, always ready for something else, something different. I was making up for lost time. I wanted one after the other after the other, I wanted it breezy and light and fast. It wasn't necessarily always fun for the other person, but their feelings, I thought, weren't my concern. I hated drama, didn't care about what their families would think or the struggle they were having coming to terms with their sexuality. I just wanted fun, and I got bored very quickly.

The truth was, I still felt uncomfortable and disoriented about lots of aspects of my gay identity. It was easy for me to befriend flamboyant men or admire drag queens; they were so *separate* from me, from my experience. But gay women presented a different challenge. Accepting them would mean accepting myself. Looking at them—at the way they dressed or acted—felt too much like looking in the mirror. And so I rejected lesbians who presented as masculine, who buzzed their heads and rode Harleys. I was turned off by unshaven legs; repulsed by hairy armpits, having been indoctrinated from a very young age that those things were undesirable (they just needed my mom and my aunt to pin them down, I thought). During parents' weekend, I saw women walking with their mom or dad, holding hands with their girlfriends. "Bullshit," I said to myself. "No parent accepts their kids like that." To admit that some parents did would have meant confronting the truth about my own. When I saw other students hosing down the sidewalk—cleaning off chalkings from Pride celebrations of National Coming Out Day—before parents weekend, I felt validated.

It took me years to see these attitudes for what they were—internalized self-hatred. You don't go your whole life feeling sinful and dirty and then one day—*poof*—become your own number one fan.

Coming to the United States—and coming out—was like the gunshot at the start of a long race. Explosive and euphoric at first, but only the beginning of many, many torturous laps, running around the same circle, trying to win my own self-respect without losing everything I loved.

THE FURTHER I got and the longer I spent away from home, the more Islam felt like not just my religion but a thing I didn't want to lose. For me, being Muslim was inextricably entwined with being Arab. For the first eighteen years of my life, I took that identity for granted. But away from my family and culture, nothing seemed as certain as this: I was an Arab Muslim woman. Being gay was a part of me, yes, but it wasn't the only part. Surely at Smith College, I thought, a place where inclusivity was the rule and acceptance was a given, I could be all three—an Arab, Muslim, and a gay woman.

Ramadan was coming up. At HWS, I had largely observed alone, skipping my lunchtime trip to the cafeteria altogether. But my first Ramadan in the United States turned out to be especially meaningful; it was strangely gratifying to summon the discipline to fast in a land that didn't cater to my fasting. In Jordan, school closes early during Ramadan; everything shuts down midafternoon so hungry and tired observers can go home and rest. At sundown, the feasting begins—first, like the Prophet (PBUH), we'd eat a date, then there was a bowl of soup, then dinner, then atayef, a sweet dumpling filled with cheese or nuts. During the year we rarely had dessert, but for Ramadan it was a nightly occurrence. In the Middle East, Ramadan has become so decadent that many people actually gain weight before the month is over. I loved the celebrations, but I also wondered if they strayed too far from the notion of sacrifice. In the United States, the sacrifice was pronounced.

I had learned about the Muslim Student Association at Smith during the international student orientation. Just the year before, I had avoided groups like this, preferring to find my own way without the burden of labels or obligation. But now the idea of sharing iftar—the meal that breaks fast at sunset—seemed appealing. Refreshing, too, I thought, to be around people to whom I didn't have to explain the very concept of iftar, the way I could talk to my gay friends about certain things that only they understood. Maybe in

America, I would find other Muslims like me. Muslims who loved their faith but who were critical of its contradictions and outdated practices.

The Muslim student group met on Wednesdays on the first floor of a nearby house, a short walk across campus from my dorm. On the way there, I shuffled through fallen leaves and the quad lit by the last purple moments of sunlight.

I found them in the living room, looking familial and cozy on couches and love seats, about a dozen women in an uneven circle. There were lots of skin tones and styles in the room, representing the racial and geographical diversity of our faith and the full spectrum of religious self-expression—hijab to shorts. I recognized one of the women from the international student orientation. I had seen the leader of the group, a hijab-wearing Pakistani woman named Amina, in Dee-Ann's dorm room; they were both head residents. Amina looked up at me as I came in, and the rest of the group fell to a hush.

"Can we help you?" she asked.

"I'm here to join," I said, thinking that much was obvious.

Amina didn't miss a beat. "This is a group for Muslims."

"I am," I answered, putting my hand on my chest. "I'm Muslim." I looked over at the woman I recognized from orientation, perhaps for some corroboration, but she just stared at the floor.

"This group isn't for you," Amina said, her voice at once friendly and firm.

It wasn't hard to figure out; somehow, through Dee-Ann or some other kind of social osmosis, Amina knew that I was gay. To her, that meant I wasn't a true Muslim. All of these women were so different—some veiled, some not; some in Western clothes, others in Muslim tunics; some with olive skin, some with brown—they were all welcome here. And I was not.

I was presented with a familiar calculation. Change their minds or change myself. But I didn't really care what Amina—or any of them—thought about my sexuality or my faith. I had come here for their camaraderie, not their approval. If they didn't want me around, why would I waste my time trying to prove that I was worthy of them, good enough? I nodded and left.

On the walk home through a now-dark campus, I thought about the bismillah, the most important phrase in Islam, the words we say before we pray, or eat, or do good deeds: Bismillah al-rahman al-raheem. *In the name of Allah, the most compassionate, the most merciful.* There was nothing compassionate or merciful about rejecting me. I would fast alone, grateful for the chance to cleanse my soul and deepen my connection to Allah.

But that night, in that tastefully arranged living room, I couldn't deny that something had shifted. Whatever hope the world seemed to hold that I could be both at once—gay and Muslim—faded as quickly as a November twilight. It certainly wasn't possible in Jordan, and, apparently, not even in a place like Smith. Something would have to change, and maybe that something was me.

CHAPTER 18
A PILGRIM

AT SOME POINT in their life, every Muslim must make a pilgrimage to Mecca. It is one of the five pillars of Islam, the things that we are obligated to do as part of our faith. Usually this is done during hajj, a journey that takes place over multiple days during the last month of the lunar calendar. An umrah, sometimes called a "hajj lite," is a shortened pilgrimage to Mecca that Muslims can take at any time of the year. Going on umrah would allow us to travel to Mecca as a family during my winter break.

The weeks leading up to the trip home were like the others—the stomachache, the tortured dreams. When my roommate said she thought she heard me crying in my sleep, I joked it was probably just one of our housemates having loud sex.

At night, to avoid the nightmares, I stayed up late reading Malcolm X's autobiography and writings. When the civil rights leader had gone on his hajj, he was transformed, inspired, he said, by a religion that allowed him, a Black man, to eat from the same plate, drink from the same glass, and sleep on the same rug as everyone else. Back in America, he wasn't even allowed to use the same bathroom. Mecca and the "one human family" he found there, "rearranged my thought patterns," he said, and brought him "numerous unexpected blessings beyond my wildest dreams."

Malcolm was my man. Unapologetically proud of who he was, outspoken about the injustices of the world. His evolution from angry activist to revered social justice warrior had inspired me to channel some of my own indignation into the LGB-rights work I did at Smith. If Malcolm X had loved Mecca, I was sure that I would, too.

Mecca is like the nucleus of Islam. It's where Muhammad (PBUH) went to destroy the false gods the Bedouins had been worshiping and delivered a new faith. There were not hundreds of greedy and capricious gods, he said, but one god—Allah—and he was compassionate and loving. Allah wanted us to love each other, to treat each other equally— that meant women and slaves, too. I had seen this story on TV every year during Ramadan, in a three-hour epic movie called *The Message*.

Every year, my brothers and I sat cross-legged on the floor and watched, waiting for the warrior Hamzah to arrive on horseback and whip out his two-bladed sword. I loved it so much I watched both the Arab and English versions, even though the actors in the English one had painted their faces a garish brown to look more Middle Eastern. (They just looked dirty.)

During those long nights poring over Malcolm X, I began to think that maybe going on umrah might change me, once and for all. That maybe going to Mecca would be like going to Oz. There, I would see—would truly *feel*—Islam in its full, glorious color. Everywhere else it had been flattened into black and white, used to hurt and oppress people. But in Mecca I would find the real Islam, and like Malcolm X, I hoped, I would receive blessings beyond my wildest dreams. I would be made straight.

WHEN THE PLANE began its descent into Jeddah, Saudi Arabia, all of the women around me began pulling out scarves like magicians. They pulled them from purses, overhead compartments, and seatback pockets. I knew this was coming, had been sure to also dress appropriately, with my ankles and wrists concealed in fabric, but it was still a surprise. I fumbled with mine, how to wrap it around my head so that none of my hair would show, which wasn't allowed in this country. I sat still as my mother expertly wrapped the cloth around my face. Next to her, Abla and Taytay were already covered.

In Saudi Arabia, they practiced a conservative Islam that I was not used to called Wahabism. I thought that it was barbaric and primitive and manipulated what Islam was truly about. Instead of a focus on love and equality, Wahabism emphasized moral purity and strict behavior and dress codes. Anyone who didn't fall in line was severely punished.

As my mom wrapped my head, I looked over at my brother, oblivious and absorbed in his Nintendo Game Boy. Meanwhile, I was struggling to put on my hijab so that men like him would not be tempted by women. The familiar heat of resentment washed over my face. I wanted to smack him and wrap the hijab around his head.

There were about thirty of us traveling together—aunts, uncles, cousins—and once we were in the airport, we all gathered around the oldest man in our family. To get into Saudi Arabia, the women would need to prove that they had a guardian, a male who would be responsible for us while we were in the country. Even my grandmother, now in her sixties, had to stand next to one of her sons to be let in.

Outside the terminal, we made our way to the private bus my father had chartered to take us into Mecca. It didn't take long for the airport to give way to the wide-open expanse of the desert. In Jordan, the desert was pink, purple, red. In Saudi Arabia, even as the sun began inching toward the horizon, the desert was so bright it was almost white.

"If we had flown in at night," said my father, who had

been on many business trips to Saudi Arabia, "you would have seen the whole country lit up." He used a sweep of his arm to suggest the entirety of it. That's how wealthy this country was. In Jordan, rich neighborhoods had street-lights, but not poorer ones, and certainly not rural areas. The only road in Amman that was consistently lit was the one to the airport.

Soon we were passing beneath the Mecca Gate, the large, illuminated archway shaped like an open Quran. A green sign read MUSLIMS ONLY. A red sign read FOR NON-MUSLIMS. This was the point at which non-Muslims would have to turn around and go back. It was surreal, and not just because the gate was lit up like a Ferris wheel. After twenty years, I was finally here, the place I had turned to my whole life to pray (when I did pray). Every day, five times a day, a billion Muslims turned their mats toward Mecca and said their prayers, hopes and wishes all lobbed this way like pennies into a fountain. I waited to feel Allah's presence permeate my very being. I looked around at my family and wondered if they could feel the magic yet.

I guess I thought it would look like the movie I had grown up watching. I thought it would be a dusty, rusty, and rough place. I thought it would be rudimentary, a place stripped down so that the essence of Islam would shine through. "One human family" embarking together on a spiritual journey.

But that is not the Mecca I found. On the outskirts of the city, I began to notice them. The tents. The encampments. The rows and rows of bodies asleep on the ground. The five pillars say that anyone who is *able* must make a pilgrimage; my family was *able* to do so in comfort. I could see that wasn't true for everybody. I could see that some people spent everything they had just to get here, believing Allah would take care of whatever hardships that necessitated.

Past the tents and heaps of pilgrims, the center of the city erupted from the desert like a glittering oasis. It was metal and marble. It was neon and fluorescent. It was a gigantic mall and a hotel as nice as any we had stayed in over the years. It was the colonel from Kentucky Fried Chicken, lit up in lurid red and grinning upon the holiest city in the world. It was futuristic and technicolor, but it wasn't Oz; it was Las Vegas.

It looked more like a tourist destination than a spiritual one, but maybe that stood to reason. Millions and millions of Muslims descended on Mecca each year; they needed a place to stay, to eat, and, I guess, to shop. That first night, I tried to ignore the thick beams of light that seeped behind the curtain after I had turned off the lamp. In the morning, we would walk into the Great Mosque, the largest mosque in the world, to orbit the Kaaba, the most sacred site in all of Islam. This simple cube-shaped structure sat in the middle of a massive open-air space that looked almost like a football stadium. The Kaaba was like our crucifix, or our Star of David: the most recognizable symbol of our faith.

MORNING CAME, AND we pulled on our headscarves, our thin white abayas; we shuffled in sandals and flip-flops across the street to enter the mosque beneath the towering hotels. At the entrance we left our shoes in a numbered cubby.

Our day would begin with salat al-fajr, the morning prayer, which took place inside one of the Great Mosque's halls, a wide room of soaring columns and arched ceilings crowded with fans. I was disappointed when the crowd almost instinctually separated—men downstairs, women upstairs. I briefly thought of Malcolm X's excitement that he was able to stand next to blond-haired, blue-eyed white people and be regarded as equal. "Equality," "oneness," "unity": he wrote these words seemingly unaware they only applied to *half* of the pilgrims in Mecca. The male half. I scolded myself to concentrate on the prayer.

I shouldn't have been surprised, though. Mosques in Jordan were also divided by gender; that was why I didn't go. I didn't want to stand behind the men or be put on a separate floor. I'd just thought that maybe in Mecca—in Malcolm X's Mecca—it wouldn't be like this. Women lumbering up the stairs, listening to the imam through a tinny speaker.

"Oh, stop it," Abla said, swatting my arm.

"Stop what?"

"Huffing! Who cares! At least we don't have to stand *behind* them." Abla rarely went to mosque in Jordan. I looked over at my mom and Taytay. I wondered if they were thinking what Abla and I were thinking. I studied my nine-year-old sister's face. What was she absorbing?

After, it was time to enter the central area of the Great Mosque, the outdoor space where we would find the Kaaba. We would walk together as a family, women linked arm in arm, men linked arm in arm, too. Just as we emerged into the sunlight, we heard a man yelling aggressively, his voice coming closer. Immediately, my aunts and female cousins began checking their head wraps, touching their foreheads to see if any hair was exposed. I saw him then, a bearded man in a red-checked kaffiyeh, holding a long switch—he was one of Saudi's infamous morality police. And he was coming directly at Taytay.

Quickly, my mom straightened her mother's scarf, covering the few strands of her hair that had become visible, and the policeman punctuated his tirade with a mean glare before walking off. My heartbeat hastened; my stomach flipped. I felt my father's hands on my shoulders. "It's okay," he said into my ear. "You're not going to do anything wrong."

But no one had done anything wrong, I thought. What did my grandmother's hair have to do with morality?

A few deep breaths and careful steps later, we had joined

our place in the parade of thousands of pilgrims circling the Kaaba. It was shrouded in a deep-black velvet fabric, with verses from the Quran embroidered in a gold thread that glowed in the sun.

To complete the ritual, called tawaf, we had to walk around the Kaaba seven times while silently chanting a prayer. On each lap, we would get closer and closer to the Kaaba, and on our last, we would touch it.

As I approached the Kaaba, I realized this might be my only chance; I needed to make my own appeal directly to Allah.

"Please forgive me," I begged silently. "Please change me."

We circled and circled.

"Please forgive me. Please change me."

We circled and circled. I dug my fingernails into my palms.

"Please forgive me."

We circled and circled.

"Please change me."

We circled. When it was our turn to touch the Kaaba, I let the tips of my fingers graze the thick, black fabric. I closed my eyes tight. I summoned every cell in my body to attention. And I begged Allah to make me straight.

"Keep moving, don't stop," Abla said, squeezing my arm with hers. I felt the breath and body odor of the thousands of people behind me, all waiting to touch the Kaaba, all hoping to have their prayers answered. Were there others? I wondered. How many were asking for the same thing as me?

WE STAYED IN Mecca for two more days, completing the other rites of our pilgrimage. We walked seven times between Safa and Marwa, two small hills now concealed in the underground section of the Grand Mosque, to re-create Hajar's desperate search for water for the infant Ishmael. One day our bus took us out onto the Plains of Arafat, a barren, rocky place where we listened to sermons and gathered stones for our next rite, which was hurling those stones at large columns within the Great Mosque that were said to represent Satan. Finally, we were driven to Medina, to worship at another impressive mosque, this one topped with ten spires and a green dome, under which the Prophet (PBUH) was buried.

All the while, I waited. For the lightning strike, the thunderclap of change that I knew would happen in my heart. Hours and days passed, and I didn't feel it. But I knew it would come. When the plane touched down in Jordan and I still felt just like me, I wouldn't give up. I wouldn't let myself think that awful thought: that maybe Muslim Las Vegas had made things worse, not better. That maybe nothing was going to change after all.

A few days later, Misty called. It was morning in Amman,

around two a.m. in Northampton. Misty had stayed up late just to call me; she insisted the maid wake me up.

"Hello?" I said, leaning against my pillow propped up against the wall.

"I saw Melissa today—" Misty began in a singsong voice.

At this, my spine straightened. "Who?"

"Um, just the girl you've been talking about for weeks. Are you hungover?"

"I don't drink."

There was a pause. "Whatever. Well, I was at the gym and so was she, with Anna, and guess what. She has knobby knees!"

"Really?"

"Yes! Her legs are skinny, and her knees are knobby. Anyway, how's it going there, and when are you coming back?"

"It's fine. On Monday. I gotta go—my mom is waiting on me," I lied. I hung up before Misty could say another word about Melissa.

Knobby knees. I was feeling straighter already.

CHAPTER 19
RHUBARB PIE AND JERRY SPRINGER

WHEN I RETURNED to Smith, my friends knew something was wrong. Quiet and withdrawn, I was not the outgoing Luma they were used to. Eventually, they would learn to recognize these periods as deprogramming—a kind of emotional whiplash from switching back and forth between worlds.

On the outside, I appeared sullen and lethargic. But on the inside, my mind was moving a mile a minute, trying to come to terms with my experience in Saudi Arabia. Back in the United States, I couldn't stop thinking about the people I had seen lined up on the hard ground of the desert, the morality police kicking people who had fallen asleep on the floor of the mosque, the lights, and the opulence a direct assault on my pilgrimage. I had always been critical of Saudi Arabia: they didn't allow women to drive, the government refused to accept refugees during the Gulf

War, Wahabism was such an extreme version of Islam it was hard to see how it related to my faith.

When I returned to Malcolm X for guidance, different lines stood out to me this time. When I reread that in Saudi Arabia, "A car, a driver, and a guide have been placed at my disposal," I slammed the book shut, disgusted by the hypocrisy.

Worst of all, I still felt the same. Torn in half. Unable to see a way forward. Gay.

Misty was less patient about my sullen mood than Dee-Ann, who told her to give me time. When a girl named Stacey yelled and stormed off while we were all watching a movie, I looked at Misty and Dee-Ann, confused.

"You idiot!" Misty scolded. "You hook up with her, and you can't even acknowledge her existence?"

"I hooked up with her?" I asked sincerely. I honestly couldn't remember it.

A few days later, Misty found me folded over on the same couch.

"We're going dancing tonight—you coming?"

"No, I'm tired," I said, not looking up. "I'm gonna stay in."

"Take a nap now, then we can go tear it up on the dance floor." Misty shook her hips for emphasis.

"I really don't feel like it."

"Melissa will be there."

"I told you, I'm straight."

It had been almost ten days since I had returned; Misty was done with patience.

"You're full of shit." Her Maine accent was coming out now. "You think you're straight because you went to Mecca?"

"Yes, actually, I do," I snapped back. "Now can you please just leave me alone?"

With the exasperated force of a mother, she grabbed my arm, yanking me from the couch.

"Hey, I was—" I said, but we were already moving toward the stairs.

"If you think you're straight, if you think your prayers were answered, let's go ahead and test it." Her voice was echoing in the stairwell. "If you're really straight, then no girl, no dance, no anything will be able to tempt you."

"Fine!" I said, tearing my arm from her grasp. "Let's go, and I'll show you."

My ten days of straightness ended a few hours later as I danced with Melissa and went home with Holly.

MISTY WASN'T JUST the first person in her family to go to an elite college, she was the first to attend college period. Her working-class family came from Kennebunk, five miles away from Kennebunkport, the coastal enclave where families like the Kennedys and Bushes owned vacation cottages.

Despite the exclusive zip code, Misty was the only one of my friends who actually had to work to pay for college. She had a work-study position and a second job, too, washing dishes in the cafeteria and bagging groceries at the local co-op. She started working two jobs the minute we got out for summer break. On that first night, when I said my father worked in steel, Misty had pegged me for a steelworker's daughter, blue-collar like her.

Of course, I was not blue-collar. I was blue-blooded. I did not have to work. My father sent me a generous monthly allowance and had given me a credit card for larger purchases. I never had to worry about buying what I needed. There was an Armani suit in my closet that Misty loved to borrow, long after she figured out my dad wasn't a steelworker.

Misty and I may have come from different classes and countries, but we had a lot in common.

We were both the oldest of four, both guarded about our families and our feelings. We were both products of proud, clannish cultures, of places fiercely skeptical of outsiders. Misty told me once that every knowable drop of blood in her body had come from Maine, and that was on purpose. It made me think of the Middle East, of how my grandparents had wanted my mother to marry a Syrian, or how my uncles could trace us back to the small minority who were 100 percent Jordanian. And here we both were, emerging cautiously into a new world, breaking out of the bubble we had been born in.

Maybe that's why Misty was good at changing the subject when someone asked about my family, or why I didn't tease her when the thick Maine accent she was so good at hiding came out after a few drinks. We never had a long conversation about what it meant to try to walk away from a tribal, insular family, but we surely recognized it in each other.

Our connection confused other people. They couldn't make sense of our match, of the straight, cherub-cheeked Mainer and the gay, dark-haired Arab. They asked if we were secretly dating, a reasonable question, since we often held hands. And they were astonished to learn that Misty had invited me home during our first summer. No one had ever met a member of Misty's family; like me, she kept her family far away from Smith and Smith far away from them.

When I told my parents I would be visiting a friend's house in Maine, my dad had a lot of questions. In Jordan it was easy; even though Amman was a big city, he could gather all the intel he needed based on last name alone. In the United States, he had no frame of reference.

"Wyman. Is that Jewish?"

"No, Dad, she's Christian."

"That sounds Jewish. You know, I had a Jewish friend in college."

"I know, Dad."

"What does her father do?"

I knew if I told my dad the truth—that Misty's father had left the family years ago—he would judge.

"I'm not sure—hey, do we have any cousins I should visit while I'm there?" It was a joke. My father had an uncanny ability to find a "cousin" almost anywhere in the world.

"Where in Maine?"

"Kennebunk."

"Kennebunkport? That is where President Bush lives!"

"He's my cousin?" I joked, deciding not to correct him.

"I hear it's beautiful. Take pictures, eat lots of seafood," he instructed.

We cut across Massachusetts and headed north on coastal backroads. Misty knew exactly which saltwater-stained shack to turn in to for my first lobster roll. Butter dripped down my chin as the gray Atlantic Ocean lapped at the rocky shoreline.

Back in the car, it was my turn to drive. We were singing some '80s classic song at the top of our lungs when I saw the swirl of red and blue lights in the mirror. My stomach lurched as I took my foot off the gas.

"Just slow down and pull over," Misty said, turning the CD player off. The wind had blown her blond hair across her forehead.

"Where? Right here?" In Jordan, people stopped their cars in the middle of the road all the time, chaos and other people's inconvenience be damned.

"Oh, no, to the right. Just off the shoulder there," she explained. I followed Misty's pointer finger and put the car into park. "Now turn off the car; he'll probably just give you a ticket."

"Why? This won't take long, right? Plus—air-conditioning?" I pointed at the vent.

"If you don't turn your car off, he'll think you're about to take off."

"Take off where?" Americans were so sensitive.

The police officer approached my window, where, thanks to Misty's instruction, I had my license and registration ready for him. For a few minutes, I nervously scratched my fingernail against the rubber of the steering wheel, waiting for him to come back. Misty was flipping through her CD case, unfazed.

When I once again heard boots against the pavement, I took a twenty-dollar bill from my wallet. Before the officer could hand me anything, I extended the money out the window.

"For the ticket," I said, nodding confidentially. I had seen my father and uncles do this a million times. I had done it myself. Everybody won in this scenario—the driver got back to their busy day and the cop got some pocket money.

The officer stepped back slightly and said, "Are you trying to bribe me, ma'am?" I felt Misty's head whip toward the driver's seat.

"She's not from here!" Misty exclaimed, touching my shoulder as if to reel my hand back into the car. "See her license? In her country they pay right away." I could tell she was making it up as she went.

"Mm-hm," the officer said, a hint of incredulity in his voice. "You'll pay this at the courthouse or through the mail, okay?" He spoke slower now, like I didn't speak English.

Back on the road, Misty and I laughed and laughed.

We drove past Ogunquit and up toward Portland. We drove through Kennebunkport, with its huge mansions, and Misty pointed out the Bush compound. Then we headed west toward Kennebunk.

Kennebunk was the opposite of its portside sister. Rural, rusty, and working-class. A small downtown and a smattering of farmhouses that dotted rolling, endless hills. As we pulled into the driveway of one of the houses—dingy-white and weathered—Misty announced we had arrived.

"We'll have more space at my grandparents'; my mom's place doesn't really have room for us," she said cryptically. I didn't ask questions.

You can tell a lot about a person by their family—I must have heard my parents say that a million times. Now I would learn exactly who Misty was, a luxury she would never have with me.

Misty's grandmother Leana was a short, sturdy woman with her gray hair pulled back to reveal deep lines carved into her forehead. She greeted us at the door and spoke quickly—I could understand almost nothing through her heavy accent, her stretched-out *a*'s and flattened *o*'s. Misty laughed and translated. "Don't worry, you'll get the hang of it in no time."

Inside, the house was spartan. Misty's grandfather was a hunter; a few of his guns hung on the walls. Otherwise, they were bare. After we dropped our bags in the upstairs bedroom we would be sharing (apparently, even Leana thought we were dating), Misty said she needed to go see some aunts and cousins.

"You can stay here and help me make pie," her grandmother offered. "And, Misty, don't forget to fill up the *caaah* with gas."

I had rarely eaten pie and never made one, so I opted to stay. Plus, I knew for a fact that grandmothers were the very best cooks.

Misty left, and Leana got busy pulling out ingredients and preheating the oven. I watched, waiting for an assignment. Finally, she took a large bucket from the fridge filled with bright pink stalks.

"Sit over there," she said, pointing to a recliner in front of the TV. I was getting better at decoding the accent and did as I was told. Leana followed me with the bucket in one hand and an empty bowl in the other. She perched on the edge of the second recliner, not two feet from mine. Before she said a word, she aimed the remote at the TV and found what she was looking for—Jerry Springer.

Leana handed me a stalk. "Start peeling," she instructed, turning her face back to the TV. "Misty just loves *rhubaahb* pie."

I was confused. This pink celery was going to be our dessert?

Leana must have noticed my furrowed brow. "Have you ever had it?"

"No, we don't have this—rhubarb?—where I'm from."

"Oh, taste it. It's wicked good."

I took a tiny nibble of the stalk in my hand; my mouth immediately cinched up from the tartness. It tasted vaguely like the sour plums we picked from Taytay's trees—but those we topped with a dash of salt. Mainers were great with lobsters, but maybe not pies, I decided.

I watched Leana peel her first stalk and then imitated the process, pulling down from the dry end of the stem, discarding the papery skin in the empty bowl. We peeled and peeled. We peeled while Leana shook her head at Jerry Springer, muttering something about loose values. We peeled, and Leana looked at me and asked, "How could you not even know who the father of your own baby is?" I was pretty sure that was a rhetorical question.

I loved watching Leana expertly peel each stalk of rhubarb. It reminded me of my grandmother rolling balls of
kibbeh. Only, my grandmother's hands were soft and small,
hands that had never had to work too hard. Leana's hands
were thick and tan, tough as rope. Maybe you could tell a lot
about people by their families, but you could learn all you
needed to know just by looking at their hands.

When we finished, Leana headed into the kitchen to
assemble the pie and get to work on dinner. I followed and
sat nearby at the kitchen table, watching. I offered to help,
but she just shook her head at me.

I could see—in that kitchen and during the entire trip—
where Misty had gotten all of the attributes I liked about her.
Her strength and independence. Her resolve to do things
her upbringing would have made impossible for other people. On that trip to Maine, I understood what it meant for
Misty—the daughter of a school bus driver and a deadbeat
dad—to not only launch herself into the moneyed world of a
Seven Sisters college, but to pay for it on her own. The most
remarkable part was that Misty never complained. Never let
it stop her from having fun or picking up the tab at the end
of the night. Breaking barriers, doing the impossible, it only
seemed to make Misty stronger.

Watching my friend make her way in the world without
the benefit of money or a stable family life made me think
for the very first time that—maybe, just maybe—I could do
it, too.

Misty returned a few hours later to find us setting the table.

"Did you fill up the *caaah*?" I asked. Misty raised her eyebrows.

At dinner I was pleased to find we were having not one, but two kinds of pie, each a first for me: shepherd's and rhubarb. Both were wicked good.

THERE WASN'T A moment when I decided I would stay in the United States for good, just like there wasn't a single instant that revealed the fact of my sexuality to me. There were the flashpoints: the bloody sheet, the honor killings, the police officer and his gun, the morality police and his switch. Slowly, I came to accept it. If I wanted to live, I couldn't go back to Jordan.

For the first few years that I was in college, I was able to relax a little bit. I had years to figure out what I would do after graduation. But by the time I traveled to Maine with Misty, I had already been weighing the options carefully, nearly constantly.

There were weeks when I'd think about asking one of my gay guy friends for a green-card marriage. There were months when I'd wonder what job I could get with my anthropology degree that would also guarantee me a work visa. I had heard of so-called "Einstein visas" offered to immigrants with talent so profound they were able to skip to the front of the immigration line. But I was no Martina Navratilova or John Lennon.

And then there was asylum. In 1994, two years before I made pie with Misty's grandmother, US Attorney General Janet Reno had issued an order that would allow homo-sexuals from other countries to seek political asylum in the United States. In order to do so successfully, you needed to first prove that you were a member of that persecuted social group and, additionally, that there was a "well-founded fear" you would be persecuted on the basis of that membership should you stay in your country of origin.

I wasn't sure how a person could *prove* that they had a well-founded fear; after all, an emotion wasn't a tangible item, like a suitcase you could just hand over for inspection. All I knew was that every time I thought of going back to Jordan for good, I thought of that police officer and the thousands just like him. I thought of the honor killings. I thought of my own death.

CHAPTER 20
PROVE IT

ALMOST A YEAR later, during the spring of my junior year, Misty and I went on another road trip, this time to Boston. Our tiny tin can of a car rocked in the wind as we sped down I-90 on our way into the city. We were singing again, this time to cover up the sound of the wind rushing through the gaps in the metal and to squelch the anxiety seeping up from our insides. We were on our way to the most important appointment of my life, to meet with an immigration lawyer about my asylum application. My mind raced faster than the wheels.

My stomach was also in bad shape. My body's answer to stress is to expel. And as soon as we parked, that's exactly what it did. I stepped around the Lucky Charms that lay scattered on the pavement to get out of the car, wiped my mouth, and nodded at my friend.

A heavy wooden door opened to a vast waiting room,

and I wiped my palms on my pants as I walked up to the reception desk. After I gave the woman at the desk my name, I took one of the hard chairs next to Misty, the nervous silence like static electricity between us. She rubbed my arm and gave me a big smile that didn't quite reach her eyes.

I had found Richard Iandoli's name in the back of the *Advocate*, a gay newspaper you could pick up for free at most bars and coffee shops in Massachusetts. When I called, I got to talk to Richard himself, who said he had taken on a few political asylum cases, but none for gay clients. It was a category that was becoming hard to ignore, as more and more people became vocal about the violence and injustices our community faced globally.

After a few tense minutes, a tall, bearded man walked into the room, looking like a young Santa Claus. "Luma?" he said, approaching me.

I stood to shake his hand and felt my insides unclench a little. Something about him eased my fear. Misty and I followed him into his office, where Richard sat behind an enormous desk, shuffled some papers, pushed his glasses up his nose, and locked me in his gaze.

"As I mentioned to you on the phone, you would probably get a better outcome if you applied in San Francisco or Canada. The Boston courts haven't really ruled favorably in asylum cases."

"I really can't," I said. My credit card didn't have a limit, but I knew my dad read his statements carefully. Flying across or out of the country would bring up questions I didn't have answers for. "My parents will know—I need to do this here."

"And you know there are . . . other ways of getting citizenship." Richard raised his eyebrows. I knew he was talking about marriage, applying for a work visa. I had considered those things, too. But at some point in the last year, I had decided that whatever happened next—whether I stayed or had to return to Jordan—that I was done with the lies. With pretending. Asylum would require renouncing my Jordanian citizenship. But at least I could finally tell the truth.

I shook my head no.

"So we'll need your testimony, but we're also going to need letters from people in your life, people who can help you prove you are gay."

"Why would that be needed?"

Richard explained that some people, desperate people, will say anything to ensure their immigration to the United States.

For a moment, I forgot to be anxious about my own immigration status. I couldn't wrap my head around it. "Why would anyone *pretend* to be gay?" I asked. It was a secret that had nearly cost me my life. I'd spent years hiding who I was, and now I would have to go to great lengths to prove it.

"The easiest way is to have a girlfriend write a testimonial," Richard said.

"Seriously?"

"Have you had one?"

Misty stifled a laugh.

"Yes, but I am not sure if any of them would write something. And I don't want to put anyone in that position anyway."

"You will have to. The more information we have, the stronger our case will be. More is better."

The double knot in my stomach returned as Richard went on about all the personal information he would need about my country, my family, and me. Things I had tried for years not to think about. Things I had tried to bury, to hide, to pray away. The thought of putting this all down on paper beckoned bile into the bottom of my throat.

I felt Misty's steady hand on my back.

Richard explained that there could be multiple rounds of the process. The first round would be an interview with an asylum officer. If the officer approved my application, the process would be over right then. But that was unlikely, he said. More often, the asylum officer denies approval, and the case moves to an appeal. At that point, I would plead my case in front of a judge and jury. The longer this went on, the more expensive it would be. The longer it went on, the more excuses I would need to come up with to keep my parents at bay.

Richard must have noticed my posture changing. "Are you sure you want to do this?"

I closed my eyes. I saw my mother on the front steps of our house. I saw Aunt Abla surrounded by potato chips on my parents' bed. I saw the olive trees in our backyard, relenting to the hot wind, the swimming pool rippling below. I saw my brothers at the breakfast table, pouring orange juice so fresh it tickled your nose. I saw my baby sister fast asleep in her crib, back when I used to rock it with my foot while I did home-work. I saw my grandmother standing in front of her flower gardens, I heard her say, *That one's not coming back.*

Of course I didn't want to do this. I had to.

"I'm leaving for Jordan in a few weeks," I told him, "for summer break before my senior year starts. Is there anything I can get for you while I'm there?"

Richard looked alarmed. "No, but you know this has to be the last time, right? It won't look good on your applica-tion if you keep willingly returning."

I nodded. It was a perfectly logical fact that made no sense at all.

CHAPTER 21
TESTIMONY

I CHOSE ASYLUM so that I could finally stop lying, but securing it meant pulling off an enormous act of deceit. If my parents had found out that I was planning to stay in the United States, they would have been on the next flight to Boston—or had one of the many "cousins" that lived in the US escort me onto a plane back home. Keeping this secret while absorbing the idea that I would never see my country, my home, again, was so overwhelming that some days it was difficult to breathe. During those last weeks in Jordan, I said silent, agonizing, permanent goodbyes to everything I knew while pretending I was fine. Every day felt like a funeral. Swimming with my sister, telling jokes, watching TV, knowing that I would never see her graduate from high school, go to her wedding, hold her newborn. I made kibbeh with Taytay, and our customary playfulness felt darkened by a massive, looming shadow slowly closing in.

I was decidedly not fine, and by the time I got back to

Northampton, my body had made that perfectly clear. I had dropped at least twenty pounds; none of my clothes fit anymore. I could hardly keep food in my stomach. I was jittery, moody, and erratic. I yelled at my housemates for stupid things. I punched the wall so hard my friend Amanda had to take me to the hospital. A few weeks later, a girl I was dating forced me to go back to the hospital, certain that my bizarre symptoms were indicative that something was seriously wrong with me. But when an exam and bloodwork turned up nothing, the doctor sent me home.

The twist in my stomach pulsed like a bomb. At times I just wanted to self-destruct. I'd go weeks not talking to any of my closest friends, staying with random women I met at parties or the bar. I drank heavily and as frequently as I could without ruining my grades. I skipped as many Sunday phone calls with my family as possible and began subtly discouraging them from buying a plane ticket for commencement. It was survival instinct. I needed to distance myself from them to make it easier—for me and for them. The inevitable funeral would soon arrive. It wasn't that I was being buried, but I was burying all of them.

Initially, my mom pushed back. I was the first of her children to graduate, she said, and she wanted to see it.

Fly fourteen hours to see me onstage for fifteen seconds? I asked. I knew my mother hated flying, regularly having to take Valium when she flew.

We'd celebrate as soon as I got home, I promised.

...

DEE-ANN HAD GRADUATED and was now living in San Francisco and working as a stringer for the Associated Press. She used her access and contacts to dig up everything my application would need about the cultural practices and legal nuances of Jordan, to help prove my "well-founded fear." She visited an organization for gay Muslims but left after unsuccessfully trying three doors, all heavily barred for security. She pored through microfiche and newspaper articles. Country documents from the CIA and State Department. The internet was barely a resource in 1997, so it wasn't a matter of just googling. She spent days working on my behalf, calling, faxing, scouring dense legal documents.

Meanwhile, I gathered letters. I asked a handful of friends I trusted and one ex for testimonies. Asking for such a favor wasn't just difficult, it was embarrassing. I wished I could keep this deeply personal process private. I didn't want anyone to feel sorry for me. I also didn't want them to blame or judge my family. My parents weren't bad or evil people. They weren't cruel. They were trapped in and products of a cruel culture, a faith that had been manipulated by men in power. It wasn't the lion I was afraid of; it was the lion's cage.

But if I had to do it, I would do it as best I could. I would gather the most impactful letters. I was the client, but in many ways, I felt like the lawyer—making my case. No one wanted this more than I did, just like no one would suffer the consequences of a bad outcome more than I would. I thought through every angle, every detail. Friends were one thing, but I needed heft, too. I needed a regional expert, so I asked my professor, the one who had refused to sign my withdrawal paper. She happened to have also consulted for the Clinton White House on the Middle East. She could speak to the culture of honor and violence in Jordan. I also needed clout, so I summoned up all my courage and asked the president of the college, Dr. Ruth Simmons, to also write a letter of support.

All the while, I thought about other people in my position, the ones who didn't have access to a renowned Middle East expert or a Seven Sisters president. Even in America, it was about who you knew. It wasn't enough to be scared for your life; you needed to prove that your life was worth saving.

I read each letter once, to make sure it would help my case. The ones from my friends were the hardest to read. I hated to learn what this experience had been like for them. That they had suffered because of me. I hated that they ever had to see me like the girl in their letters.

Luma does not talk about home very often. When she does, it is not with hatred. It is of memories like we all have of our childhood, some good and others bad. There is a big part of Luma which will miss Jordan very much. Repeatedly, she talks of her family and how important her family is to her. She loves her country and her family and the culture she was raised in. But she knows that that culture will not allow people like her, lesbians. Luma is a lesbian, she knows nothing else and feels nothing else. She knows that the core of Luma will die if she has to go back. I sit through many hours of tears and anger over this decision.

I know that if Luma could change her sexuality and marry the man that her parents are expecting her to marry, she would. I know that if Luma thought in any way that she could live as a heterosexual, she would go home without question. The problem is that she knows she cannot. She loves her country, her country does not love her back.

Luma and I have worked together on many political projects, rallies, workshops, and activities within the lesbian community. However, Luma's most important role in my life has always been as my friend. Before returning to Jordan over breaks and vacations, I have watched her stop eating because anxiety causes her to vomit whatever food she tries to keep down. I have watched her lose dangerous amounts of weight. I have watched her stop sleeping for weeks, suffering nightmares when she tries. Perhaps most frightening, I have watched helplessly while a caring and loving friend simply "shuts down," dissociating to the point that she cannot remember simple conversations that took place days or hours earlier.

Luma, as well as I, comes from a country that excuses murders of women as crimes of honor if they feel that the murder is justified. An example of this would be a brother killing his sister simply for having a boyfriend. That is a "crime of honor" and nothing is done to the brother because he was fighting for the honor of his family. It is a culture and country that believes blood cleanses sin.

Each time, for approximately one week before the trip, she is plagued by physical ailments, mood swings, and sleeplessness. Physically, she vomits constantly, wrenching upheavals with severe stomach pain, headaches, and bowel movements. These episodes are daily, every morning. Emotionally, Luma becomes moody because she is tired. Her nightmares are so intense because they are so realistic. I sleep next to Luma, unable to hold her through her demons, but able to understand through her sleep talking that she is replaying, again and again, those events which are the reason she cannot in good conscience go back to Jordan. She cries, mutters "stop" and "no" and breathes as if she is running.

Luma comes from a very powerful and influential Jordanian family. Her family is incredibly well-known and feared. Throughout the country there is mention of the Mufleh family. This is due to the fact that Arab families basically function like a tribal culture. Certain families are feared because of their status, which is based on wealth and power. Families such as the one Luma comes from are incredibly respected and feared and as a family only allow their members to marry into a family that is of equal status. When Luma's cousin passed away due to a car accident, everybody knew about it, to the extent that King Hussein went to the funeral.

As a journalist with the Associated Press in San Francisco, I've had the opportunity to learn about political asylum. I understand the complexity of the issue and the need for careful scrutiny of cases. Knowing this, I am convinced that Luma needs asylum in order to live the kind of life she deserves.

Part of what convinced me was my search for materials to help build her case. San Francisco is a Mecca of another kind—a gay Mecca. Still, exhaustive searches of gay bookstores turned up little on the condition of lesbians in the Middle East. A letter I wrote to the San Francisco–based Arabic Society, one of the country's only organizations for gay Arabs, was returned to me unopened. A phone message to a Lebanese women's studies professor at the University of California at Davis went unanswered: a lawyer later told me that she suspected the professor was Muslim and homophobic. A visit to the International Gay and Lesbian Human Rights Center revealed tighter security than the city jail.

I searched the Associated Press for articles on the conditions of gays in Jordan, sure there would be some information in the millions of articles stored in the company's archives. A computer search uncovered 11,342 articles mentioning "homosexuality," none were listed under "homosexuality" and "Jordan." I was on the verge of calling the AP bureau in Amman when a friend advised me to check the correspondents' names. They were Muslim—better not risk it.

The task has been a daunting one, but it would be impossible not to try. Luma is one of my closest friends, and knowing her has expanded my horizons in ways I've never even told her. Until I met Luma, I had few gay friends and was ambivalent about gay rights. Now, though, I bristle when I hear a term like "lifestyle choice." With everything she has gone through and everything she has at stake, no one could believe Luma would choose to be gay. Yet she has shouldered this burden with bravery, strength, and even a sense of humor.

There is so much at stake in this case, for Luma and for all of us who care for her. Returning Luma to Jordan is as good as a death sentence. But in the United States she can live

freely and without constant fear. You must not take this place
away from her.

Economic grievances have persuaded many Jordanians to join
a variety of Muslim political groups, and the country's structural
and fiscal limitations force the king to deploy stratagems
to deflect attention away from the population's economic
hardships. As long as the king cannot address the economic
grievances of the Muslim political forces, he attempts to please
them in other ways. This has led to a substantial amount of
deference to their lifestyle demands. While Jordan's political
system may appear more open, social behavior has become
more carefully scrutinized. Such an approach presents problems
for women who may wish for greater freedom and certainly
endangers gays and lesbians whose sexual practice Muslim
religious doctrines condemn. In the Muslim world, intolerance
against gays and lesbians has increased since the Middle Ages
and has intensified with the rise of fundamentalist Muslim
organizations. Homosexuality is socially unacceptable and
punishable by law. More importantly, gays and lesbians, if
discovered, are exposed to all sorts of informal persecution.
Members of elite families virtually risk their lives if their
sexual orientation becomes known because their parents place
a higher priority on family honor than on individual freedoms
even for their own children. Families which impose punishments

on relatives for dishonorable behavior are rarely prosecuted by the state for breaking the law.

Thus, if Luma were to return to Jordan, she would have to hide her sexuality or risk death and would undoubtedly be forced to marry. Given her family's social status, she could not live outside of their control.

FINALLY, IT WAS time to write my testimony. To distill my fear and desperation into a few compelling pages, to prove that my life was worth saving.

This is my story, and I write this now because I know I have no other option. I cannot choose not to marry, so I will be forced to marry. I will be forced to marry a man. I will be forced to have sex with a man. And if I do not do what my family wants me to do, I will be killed. These seem like exaggerations, something out of a novel, something beyond the grasp of reality. This is not an exaggeration, this is not a novel, this is my life.

Sometimes I wish I had a choice. A choice of being straight. Because if I had the choice, I would choose not to dishonor my family. I would choose not to be raped by a husband. I would choose not to be killed by my family and my government. I would choose to live in Jordan.

. . .

IN JANUARY OF my senior year, five months before graduation, I drove back to Boston and delivered everything I had gathered to Richard.

"Wow, this is a lot."

"More is better," I reminded him.

I felt confident in my application even though Richard warned me not to get my hopes up. Prepare for appeals, he said. No one had won on the first try.

On the days I could keep my mind from the dark places it liked to wander to, I felt a strange new optimism, an ability to imagine a future, and the pride of possibly setting a precedent that might help others win their own asylum.

"Someone has to be the first," I told Richard.

CHAPTER 22
INTERROGATION

I WAITED. FOR four months, I waited. All around me, friends and classmates made plans, secured internships, signed leases in cities all over New England. While they touted their skills and strengths to potential employers and grad schools, I prayed my asylum application had properly conveyed just how scared and helpless I was. My friends got to show how awesome they were; I had to show how pathetic I was. To buy a few extra weeks and pay my legal fees, I got a summer job at Smith, where I would stay long after everyone else had left campus. And I waited. Frozen. Stuck. Uncertain.

Commencement arrived, and I spent another graduation ceremony trapped in my own head, detached from the celebration around me. This time I was hungover, still nursing a bruised ego from the night before, when a pretty sophomore with curly hair wouldn't give me the time of day.

And unlike my high school graduation, this time my family wasn't in the audience; there were no friendly eyes or baby sister to find in the crowd. I was, by my own design, alone. The fact of their absence was sad, but I had to focus on me now. I had to take care of myself.

"If you don't want to be criticized, don't say anything, don't do anything, and don't be anything," the commencement speaker said. How I wished to say, to do, to be nothing.

Finally, Richard called. My hearing was scheduled for May 28, ten days after graduation. Misty wanted to come; Dee-Ann said she'd fly in. But I just wanted to be alone, without the distracting support and sympathy of my friends. I used the same arguments that had successfully kept my parents away from graduation. *No need to waste time or money,* I told them. *It will just be my attorney, the hearing officer, and me alone in a room.*

Back to Boston I went, the scenery a blur in my periphery. I forced my mind into some kind of meditative state; I don't think I changed lanes for two hours. I pretended like I was preparing for a soccer game. Giving myself pep talks, practicing my prepared answers, visualizing victory.

The immigration court was buried deep in the spiraling streets of downtown Boston. I maneuvered my rental car into a pay lot and found Richard waiting at the front door of the courthouse. Side by side, we made our way to the appointment, a small room on the first floor with nothing inside but three chairs, a small table, and a tiny window near the ceiling. It looked like an interrogation room. My body felt jittery and clumsy as I lowered myself onto the cold plastic seat. My breath felt trapped in my rib cage.

Richard placed his briefcase on the floor and removed a few files, a pad of paper, and a pen. He wouldn't be able to interject or object during this meeting; he was only there to observe and take notes to prepare for the appeal he believed was inevitable. This was my hearing and mine alone.

Soon, we heard the staccato click of heels on tile. The door opened, and in walked a stern-looking woman in a gray skirt suit, her hair in a short bob. This was my asylum officer, Ann McPhee. I felt the tiny window shrinking behind me. My fate was in her hands.

As she sat down and readied her things, I tried to read this woman, tried to imagine which part of my story would resonate with her. Did she have kids? Did she know any Muslims? Was she a feminist—or at least a woman who believed another woman shouldn't be forced to marry? Was anyone in her family gay? But nothing about Ann McPhee gave me any clues. Her clothes were nondescript, her makeup modest. If we had been in her office, I could have scanned the bookshelf or the photos on her desk. There was a reason we were alone in the sterile room. In here, we weren't supposed to be full, dynamic human beings. We were legal entities, and the business between us wasn't about our families or our feelings or our favorite things; it was about the law.

"Why do you want to leave Jordan?" she asked first.

"I don't *want* to," I said slowly. Richard had advised me to be very deliberate in my answers. "It is unsafe for me to go back."

"Even here, Miss Mufleh, being gay is not fully accepted. People still get beat up. People still get harassed."

"Yes, but here the government cannot kill you for being gay. Those who commit those crimes will be arrested. In Jordan, I *am* the crime."

Ann McPhee's eyes narrowed. She looked skeptical.

"That makes it very different," I reiterated.

For an hour, she pelted me with rapid-fire questions. About my family, my parents, my plans for the future.

"Do your parents hit you?"

"No."

"Do any members of your family hit you? Your brothers or uncles?"

"No."

"And what are you going to do if you get to stay in the United States?"

"I don't know. I haven't allowed myself to think about that."

"So you had that one incident in the park when you felt threatened?"

"Yes."

"Why did you feel threatened?"

"The gun . . . I don't know, it was scary."

"Scared but not *harmed*?"

"No."

Richard scribbled page after page on his legal pad. My stomach was heavy, and my head hurt. I felt a year's worth of exhaustion pulling on the skin beneath my eyes.

Then Ann McPhee returned to the same question she started with. "Why do you want to leave Jordan? If your life is in danger, like you say, then why have you returned"—she checked her notes—"seven times in the last three years?"

"I never said I *wanted* to leave." I was close to my breaking point; I could feel the rage collecting in my chest. Biting my bottom lip to keep my mouth closed, I pushed my chair back and left. I needed air.

As soon my back hit the brick wall outside, Richard emerged from the building. "You have to go back in," he said, his voice betraying something that sounded a lot like panic. Behind his glasses, his eyes were wide. He reached out to touch my arm but stopped, as if he was unsure how I might react.

"I can't," I said, swallowing tears. "I keep going back because I don't want to say goodbye to them."

This time, Richard didn't stop himself. He gathered me into a big Santa Claus hug. "I know. Let's just try and go back in there and finish it off."

"How much longer?" I asked into Richard's jacket, the heat of my breath warm on my face.

"I don't know."

There would be an appeal, I thought. How I would get through it, or afford it, or finagle more time in America, I didn't know.

"Okay. I'll go back in."

Richard kept his hand on my back as we walked down the hallway—maybe to comfort me, maybe to stop me from bolting.

"I'm sorry," he said to Ann McPhee as we resituated ourselves at the table. "As you can imagine, this is very difficult for my client."

"No. I'm sorry," she responded, looking at me. "I'm just trying to do my job, and one of the things I have to do is make sure you're telling the truth. You'd be surprised how many people lie to come to this country." The sun streamed in from the window over my shoulder; I realized Richard and I had been talking directly above it. Ann McPhee had heard our entire exchange.

"I am not lying," I said, holding back the many things I wished I could say to my asylum officer in that moment. Mostly, I wanted to ask her what it would take for her to leave *her* home, *her* family, everything that *she* loved. To make her understand this was not an impulsive, whimsical choice, but rather the most consequential decision of my life.

Ann McPhee relented five minutes and a few questions later. Richard walked me to my car in silence. As I unlocked the driver's side door, he said kindly, "It went well."

The drive back to Northampton was the opposite of the one to Boston. My hands shook on the wheel while I replayed the interview over and over. I cursed myself for all the things I hadn't said, for all the things I hadn't said right. I knew I had messed up—I let my temper get the best of me. Why had I stormed off? My mom was right: she had scolded me so many times for getting angry with my brothers. I missed her. And Taytay and Abla. I wished I could call and hear their voices, I wished I could tell them how scared I was. Once again, I ached for the impossible: to have them and to be me.

ANN MCPHEE HAD thirty days to make her decision. For the first few weeks, I was able to compartmentalize. To do my work, to check the mailbox, and when there was no decision letter inside, to go to bed. To ignore the dark cloud always overhead. But by day twenty, I was in a constant state of heart-pounding panic. The mailbox became an object of dread and obsession. I called Richard's office every morning as soon as I knew he would be there. He told me the longer it took, the less likely my application would be approved, like a jury deliberation. Assume the worst and prepare for the appeal, he said.

On day thirty, wired and nearly catatonic with anxiety, I walked into the campus mail room, turned the key in the small rectangular slot, and saw it. The letter. The space around me ceased to exist. The whole world was just me and this manila envelope.

Outside on the curb, I slid my index finger beneath the flap of the envelope. Carefully, I removed the piece of paper that would reveal my future.

My eyes scanned past the clutter of words to find the ones that mattered: *recommended for approval.*

Just then, a woman my age walked by. Seeing the tears streaming down my face, she offered a kindhearted nod. She probably thought the paper in my hands was a breakup letter. In a way, I guess it was.

Some losses are so big, so catastrophic, they cannot be contained in a single instant. They happen over and over again, rippling out into the future so that—just like that sunny summer afternoon alone on the curb in Northampton, Massachusetts—the very happiest moments of your life are also the very saddest.

CHAPTER 23
THE GOLDEN CHILD

WHEN I WAS little, a year or so before I corralled Tom the sheep into my grandfather's living room, I had my picture taken with King Hussein. It was his idea; depending on which side of my family you ask, he either wanted to get a photo with a grandchild from the Mufleh tribe (because Jiddo Riyad was a trusted advisor) or the Tabbaa tribe (because Taytay's father was a prominent Syrian merchant and, legend has it, the recipient of the first Jordanian passport). What no one ever mentioned is that there were lots of those grandchildren there that day, but for some reason the king reached his arms around my tiny waist and pulled me close.

The chosen one.

We were at the Royal Automobile Club, an exclusive establishment in the seventh circle of Amman, to watch a rally car race. My family spent a lot time at the club when

I was growing up; it's where I took tennis lessons and went swimming or bowling with my friends. On that Saturday afternoon, we had gathered to watch the cars line up before they roared out into the desert to conjure dust clouds and carve wild tracks in the sand.

King Hussein was a big fan of the sport—everybody knew that. Everybody knew about many of the king's pastimes: the cars, the karate. His personal life was very much of interest to Jordanians, who adored their ruler as if he were their beloved father. Hussein had a benevolent smile and a paternalistic charm that allowed him to keep a steady grip on power, even in an often-tumultuous country.

I don't remember that day, but it would be easy to think that I did, I've heard the story so many times. In the photo, the king is smiling, his salt-and-pepper hair fading to fuzz on the top of his head. My arm is folded over his hand, which rests gently on my ribs. My curly hair is pinned back by two blue barrettes, and I am grinning, just barely, my delicate lips turned up at the corners. Behind us, Queen Noor's hair shines in the sun.

Even when the photo wasn't that old, it looked like an antique, the light in it tinged rosy and sepia. It seemed to glow from within.

The golden child . . .

My parents cherished the photo so much they framed two copies, commemorating the king's embrace in both the living room and their bedroom. Each set of my grandparents also displayed the photo prominently in their homes, and many of my aunts and uncles did as well. There was likely never a day that went by when I didn't see the photo of the king and me.

. . . on a pedestal.

Being the favorite earned me more gifts, bigger gifts. The piano before I knew how to play one. The Mercedes before I was old enough to drive. But the expectations felt just as outsized. And as I got older, they felt crushing. Sometimes I wished it were one of my brothers in the picture. Sometimes I imagined drawing devil horns above my head. Sometimes I wondered what would happen to all those photos when everyone finally learned the truth about me.

I wasn't the golden child; I was the black sheep. And soon I would be their sacrificial lamb.

CHAPTER 24
DISCONNECTED

A FEW WEEKS after my asylum decision, I sat on the floor of Dee-Ann's apartment in Detroit, where she had moved after a promotion. It was a Friday. My summer job at Smith had ended, and my parents expected me back by Monday. Instead of packing for Jordan, I had rented a U-Haul, filled it up with books and clothes, and driven west.

I thought maybe I would stay with Dee-Ann for a while. Look for a job, think about grad school. But before I could really begin this new life, there was one thing left for me to do.

"Maybe they'll be supportive," Dee-Ann said.

"They won't," I told her. I knew it was impossible for my friend to imagine—parents turning their backs on their own child. There was no way I could explain to her how important family honor was in our culture, how it took precedence over everything—even members of the family itself. I couldn't allow myself to even imagine them saying, *It's okay, habibti, we love you anyway and we are all going to move to be with you.* Some fantasies are too dangerous to even entertain.

That night, with Dee-Ann's cat purring in my lap, I dialed the numbers on the back of a calling card. I dialed the pin. I dialed my home phone number.

Saeed, now eighteen years old and about to be a military cadet, answered.

"Is Baba there?" I asked him.

"Yeah," he said. "Hey, did you get the Nikes I asked for?"

"Saeed, I need Baba."

"The right size, right?"

"Put Baba on the phone. Now." I didn't want to lose my nerve and definitely didn't care about the sneakers I never bought.

The phone went quiet; in the background I heard my brother say my name. And then my father's voice was in my ear.

I spoke to him in Arabic until I ran out of words. Finally, I said it: "I'm gay." I said it again and again. "I'm not coming back. I don't want to live in Jordan. I can't live in Jordan."

"You are not my daughter," my father said, and I knew he meant it. I had been disowned.

In the background, I heard my mother tell Ali, Saeed, and Inam to go to their rooms, and then she was on the phone, too.

"What nonsense is this?" She sounded angry. "Who is playing with your head?"

"No one's playing with my head, Mama. I'm gay. I always have been."

"This is crazy. You are not yourself—you come home right now."

"I'm gay. And you knew it. How could you not know it?"

The line went dead. They were gone.

That night Dee-Ann and I saw a movie, *G.I. Jane*, about a woman who shaves her head and joins the US Navy, kind of like my old hero, Khawlah. Afterward, I used my dad's credit card before he could cancel it to buy Dee-Ann a housewarming gift, a toaster.

THE NEXT MORNING, I woke up feeling empty and dazed. I called a friend back at Smith to let her know I had made it to Detroit and talked to my parents.

"I couldn't get ahold of you," she said, sounding strangely worried.

"It's not that big of a deal. It was a phone call, and it went exactly how I thought it would."

She cut me off. "Luma, you don't understand. They are looking for you."

"Who is looking for me?"

"The FBI. They were here. On campus."

I felt the muscles in my shoulders contract. "What are you talking about?"

"They're saying you've been kidnapped," she said. "Just call the dean's office. They were in there for a while. No one knows how to get ahold of you."

I hung up and dialed the dean's office. At first, the secretary tried to take a message. But when she found out it was me, she put Dr. Tamzarian, the dean of international students, on the line.

He assured the FBI that I wasn't kidnapped, wasn't on drugs, wasn't in a cult. "But they want you back. And they are going to keep looking for you. Your family knows people in high places," he told me, as if I didn't know. Jiddo Riyad, and therefore my father, had a direct line to the royal palace. The king of Jordan was someone the American government liked to keep happy.

I swallowed hard and placed the phone back on the hook. As that old fear crept back into my body, I considered my options. Clearly, my parents were angry and determined to get me back to Jordan, regardless of whatever danger might wait for me there. And the only thing I had to protect me was my recently issued asylum decision, a measly piece of paper. I thought of my grandfather's stern face, my father next to him, my uncles lined up behind him. I had tried to plan for worst-case scenarios, but never in all of my planning did I imagine my family would call in a political favor or get the FBI involved. Obviously, they would stop at nothing. There were no options, really. I had to hide.

I found Dee-Ann in the living room, reading and sipping coffee.

"They're looking for me," I told her. "I have to go."

First, we went to the ATM, where I withdrew all the money left in my account: three hundred dollars. Then we went to the Greyhound station. I bought five tickets with the still-functioning credit card. Diversions. I paid for my real ticket in cash.

THE FIRST LEG took me from Detroit to Cleveland.

When we pulled into the station, I followed the swarm of people disembarking, not sure where I would go next. Inside the terminal, I realized there wouldn't be another bus until morning. I wandered the nearby streets aimlessly. It was a hot August night; a nearly full moon made shadows on the concrete. I found a group of homeless people beginning to settle in for the night beneath an overpass. I was so tired. My stores of adrenaline had given out. I found a spot on the ground, hugged my duffel bag, and fell into a deep sleep. The shuffling of shoes in the predawn hours roused me. Before I peeled myself from the concrete, I thought of my family. It was midafternoon in Jordan; I could see them lounging by the pool, laughing and eating.

I went back to the station. I bought a ticket for another unfamiliar place. My cash was slowly dwindling.

I stayed on a bus for days, seeing the United States, my new home, from an oversized, dirty window, sitting next to people I assumed were like me: people running away from something, people with nowhere to go. When one ride was over, I'd buy a couple Cokes, a couple Snickers—quick and easy calories—and another ticket. Sometimes I would see signs for cities I knew the names of, but more often I was lost. I reasoned that if I didn't know where I was, no one else could either. Maybe because I had watched too many James Bond movies, or maybe because I had grown up in a surveillance state, but this fugitive behavior came naturally to me. Lying low, hiding out—I knew how to do that.

When I remember those long hours, shivering cold, despite the summer heat, I think of worn-out mothers clutching their babies, shuffling down the aisle to the foul and claustrophobic bathroom. I think of the man who was only trying to be kind, to pull the jacket that had fallen back over me as I slept—"Everything is okay, no one is going to hurt you," he said—as I took my hands from his neck. I wanted so badly to believe him. It seemed that everyone on that bus was running from something.

Days passed, maybe weeks. I don't really know. Every once in a while, I'd make some phone calls using a prepaid card. (Using the card and keeping calls to under a minute was certainly the influence of too much James Bond.) Richard told me the FBI had shown up at his office, too. Dee-Ann told me an uncle of mine (following my credit card trail, apparently) had called and asked her to meet him at the Ritz in Dearborn. She'd refused. Finally, I called Misty. Misty knew me better than anyone, and I trusted her. She told me to meet her in Atlanta—she had a plan. I was going to join her in the mountains of North Carolina, where she was working at a diner the aunt of a friend owned.

"Are you crazy? I am not coming up to a redneck mountain town in the middle of nowhere."

"You'll blend in. You look white—people won't even notice you."

"I don't know."

"There are two ways up the mountain and two ways down. Anyone who doesn't belong there will be spotted a mile away. Arabs, FBI agents. Nobody up there trusts the government; you'll be in good hands." It sounded like my kind of town.

To be in good hands was all that I wanted. The aftershock of the past month still echoing in my brain, I needed someone I trusted to make decisions for me. I was done with tough choices for a while.

CHAPTER 25
REFUGE

I ARRIVED IN Atlanta a shell of myself—skinny, hungry, dirty. After weeks of sticking to the shadows and sitting low in my seat, the neon lights of Atlanta felt loud and chaotic, jarring after the silence and monotony of the Greyhound bus. It wasn't long before an SUV rumbled into the station, Misty in the passenger seat.

"You look terrible," Misty said with a smile. She walked around the front of the SUV and pulled me into a hug.

"Thanks."

"You look great, honey. You just need to get a good meal, maybe a piece of cake, and you'll be back to normal," said the driver, who was by now next to us, an ample woman with tight gray curls that she had teased up tall and proud.

"You must be Miss Sara." I stretched out my hand to say hello, but Miss Sara pulled me into her bosom.

"This is how we do it in the South," she said while I wondered if I had made a big mistake; I am not a hugger. "Now, let's go to the Varsity!"

Misty frowned and shook her head at me. She knew all about the infamous Atlanta burger joint—and my sensitive stomach.

Feeling ambivalent, I let Miss Sara order for me.

"Burger?"

I nodded.

"Cheese?"

I nodded.

"Fries?"

I nodded again.

"Hot dog?"

"Only if it's not pork."

At this, she eyed me skeptically. I would soon find out that pig flavored everything in the South.

"And you have to have the orange drink."

"Okay," I said with a nod.

A few minutes after I finished the meal, I was in the bathroom, Misty right behind me. "I warned you!"

"How did you warn me?" I asked from the stall.

"I shook my head!"

"That was warning me?! Plus, I couldn't be ungrateful. She was so excited about taking us to eat."

"Well, you didn't have to eat everything on the menu."

"She ordered for me!"

"Did you notice what she ordered for herself?" I could hear the satisfied smile on Misty's face. Miss Sara hadn't ordered a single greasy item.

Back in the car, when Misty turned around to offer me the bottle of Dramamine, I shook my head no. I never got motion sick. But about an hour into our ride up the mountain, I started to feel queasy. Miss Sara's feet could hardly reach the pedals—the leather seat threatened to swallow her whole—but she drove the massive SUV like Cruella DeVil, maneuvering around hairpin curves at breakneck speeds. She spent half of the journey with her head turned toward the back seat, seemingly oblivious to the terror on my face. Perhaps I should have stayed on the bus.

Miss Sara was a Southerner through and through. Before we left Atlanta, she'd named for me all the bright lights of the city, tapping the glass with her fingernails as we passed each one: CNN, World of Coca-Cola, the Varsity. She'd extolled the virtues of Krispy Kreme and grape soda and could recite a fact for every exit on the highway. Unabashedly proud of her home, Miss Sara saw me as a potential convert.

Now, with the window rolled down to ease my nausea, the smell of the mountains came drifting in: warm soil, trees in full bloom, bracingly clean air. It pushed through my dirty hair and set the straps on my duffel bag spinning.

We passed turnoffs for places called Mountain City

and Sky Valley before we finally reached our own idyllic-sounding destination: Highlands, North Carolina. Miss Sara owned a restaurant—the Mountaineer—in Highlands, a tourist town of fewer than one thousand residents. Its picturesque main street was bookended by fancy old inns, the kind with rocking chairs on columned front porches. In between were boutiques, art galleries, a bookstore. Most of the people that strolled the town's leafy sidewalks were second-home owners from Atlanta or Charlotte who drove up the mountain for a reprieve from their busy schedules. The locals you could tell by their plain clothes, their Southern drawls. It was millionaires and nobodies, and I had switched teams: I was a nobody.

By the time we got to Miss Sara's condo, it was late. It had been days—I honestly didn't know how many—since I had taken a shower. I stood under the hot water for a long time, feeling the layers of the road wash away. The grubby bus terminals, the crusty upholstery, the sticky bathroom floors. That night, on the couch, surrounded by photos of Miss Sara's cherished "grandbabies," I slipped into the kind of sleep I hadn't had for months, waking up only once to a nightmare. It was the same dream every time: a chase, a violent capture.

When I woke up, the condo was still. Miss Sara and Misty had gone to work. I walked slowly through the dim condo past the velvety recliner, past the clusters of picture frames. I paused in front of the living room window to peer through the blinds. The Appalachian Mountains rippled blue and purple to the horizon. I felt hidden. I went back to bed.

When I woke up again, I called Richard from a pay phone down the street. He answered on the first ring.

"I'm fine," I assured him. "I'm in North Carolina with a friend."

"You need to check in with me every day, okay?" he said. "I told them if they don't leave you alone, we will go to the media."

The word *them* made me cringe. I didn't want to go to the media. I had already aired enough of my family's dirty laundry in my asylum application.

After the call, I sat down in front of the computer in the corner of the living room. I held my breath as it booted up, hoping Miss Sara was the rare older woman with an internet connection. Lucky for me, she was.

Mama and Baba, I wrote. *I am fine. I am safe. Don't worry about me.*

I clicked send, knowing that between Richard's threat and my assurance, my parents would back off. I was so sure, I willed myself to forget the password to my account. I don't think I ever checked it again.

For days, Miss Sara and Misty came and went while I sat in front of the TV. Coverage of Princess Diana's death saturated every channel, and I watched with a detached interest, wondering whether the outpouring of grief was about the woman, or just who everyone wanted the woman to be. Mostly, though, I felt dull and adrift, as if lost at sea. The past was gone. The future unimaginable.

"Time to go to work, honey," Miss Sara announced one day, blocking my view of the television.

"Really? I've never worked at a restaurant."

"Claudia called in sick, so you'll have to figure it out." She snatched the remote from the coffee table, pressed the power button, and gave me one of her Blanche Devereaux smiles. She was mischief and wisdom combined, the best kind of trouble.

MISS SARA HAD a Mississippi twang that could disarm a dictator and said "bless your heart" like a mantra. After spending the early part of her life working for a Southern Baptist church, Miss Sara had moved to North Carolina and opened the diner. When the diner began taking up most of her time, her churchgoing suffered, so she decided to make the restaurant her ministry. People seemed drawn to her for comfort and guidance; they reminded me of the many lost souls who used to show up at Taytay's door.

Retro without trying to be retro, the Mountaineer was one of the only places in town where locals and tourists mixed.

The building was long and narrow; gray booths lined each wall with a row of tables sandwiched in between. Walking into the diner was like stepping back in time. Thick, ceramic mugs steamed atop laminate. There was no music—just the steady din of happy conversation. The smell of fried chicken, fried bacon, fried liver, and onions saturated everything. Pretty soon all the clothes I owned smelled like the Mountaineer.

To residents, the diner was comfortable; to tourists, it was quaint; and for Miss Sara, it was a way to help people in need. I was just one in a long line of women she had hired who needed a fresh start, a place to crash, and a paycheck. She called us "my girls," and I was happy to be one of them. Saying my name was too unusual for folks in a place like Highlands. Worried what the locals might think about an Arab in their midst, Miss Sara baptized me "Liz." Just an ordinary white girl making some money off the scores of summer tourists and autumn leaf-lookers who poured into town. I was hopeful—my skin is light and my accent non-existent; I think it gave Miss Sara a thrill to be a part of a covert operation. (She was the only one who couldn't get it right and ended up calling me "Luma-Liz" most of the time. Miss Sara would have made a terrible spy.)

As a Smith graduate, I imagined Miss Sara might ask me to manage the Mountaineer or run the cash register. But when I arrived for my first day of work, she led me through the back door, past the dumpster and the designated smoke-break spot. Inside, the kitchen was compact, still clean from the night before. We passed the prep table, the grill, and the heart of the restaurant—the deep fryer—before arriving at the stainless-steel double sink, where a coiled-up industrial faucet swayed from above. Miss Sara placed the sprayer into my hand and spoke plainly: "Scrape off the food. Hose down the dish. Load it onto this tray. Pull the handle down to lock and start the dishwasher. Repeat."

A couple of waitresses marched into the kitchen wearing old-school diner outfits. The one in blue had a permanent scowl. The one in pink had a condescending grin. They both had gray hair and black, nonslip sneakers on. I would find out later that these women were sisters. Lil (short for Lillian) and Teen (short for Christine) pretty much ran the Mountaineer. They got to pick their tables—the booths closest to the kitchen (less walking) and the booths by the windows (they were always the first to be seated)—and the other waitresses chose from the rest. Teen regularly snatched up any spare change left on tables meant for other waitresses, including Lil. Teen had diabetes and a habit of sneaking away for something sweet that her sister would later scold her for eating. The other women referred to them as *Leen, the two-headed monster.*

"Can she keep up?" Lil mumbled to Miss Sara, as if I couldn't hear. "It's gonna be busy today."

"Of course she can keep up! She's a college graduate!"

Lil was quick to dismiss the vote of confidence. "Claudia's the only one that can do this job right. This one won't last."

"Get back to work, honey." Miss Sara's *honey* meant something different every time she said it.

"It just ain't no good," Lil said, shaking her head and shuffling off. It was a phrase that she would utter dozens of times a day, I learned, whether the cooks were too slow, a waitress called in sick, or the new girl looked incompetent. *It just ain't no good.*

Miss Sara refocused her attention on me. "Every few hours, I want you to go into the restrooms—both restrooms, now—clean out the trash, wipe everything down. And, honey, be careful in the men's room; it can get a little . . . smelly." She gave me a confident nod, handed me the mop and bucket she had been holding, and then disappeared into the dining room. I stood alone at the sink and took a deep breath.

While I dipped the mop in the bleach water, I thought of the older waitresses. They assumed I was a spoiled brat, I thought, that I didn't know what it meant to work hard. They were wrong. I could be good at this. I *would* be good at this.

The front door jingled with the day's first customer.

It was all I could do to get one load of dishes in the machine before another towered in the sink. Gray dishwater pelted my face and dampened my hair. Every hour, I dutifully walked to the bathrooms with sanitizer and a fresh garbage bag in my hand. I refilled the soap and wiped down the fixtures. Sometimes I would catch a glimpse of myself in the mirror. I looked skinny and tired. My parents' voices echoed in my head.

You've been wearing the same clothes all week, my mom would say. *You can at least put some makeup on and cover your puffy eyes.*

A Mufleh cleaning a toilet! my father would chime in. *This is the life you want? To clean up other people's shit? Your grandfathers worked hard—just so you could go clean other people's shit.*

The lunch shift ended; Lil and Teen left. The dinner shift began. And it started all over again. Twelve hours of hard, repetitive labor. It was the therapy I didn't know I needed. No memories to avoid, no decisions to make, no time to think. Just a job to do. And I was good at it.

At the end of the evening, we all convened in the dining room, and someone flipped the sign to CLOSED. Outside, the sky and the mountains were the same shade of dusty black. Miss Sara counted money from the till, and I slid into the booth next to Misty, who had been just as busy as me, waiting tables. The tabletop was cool against my sweaty arms. I looked at her and smiled. It had been so long since I'd felt a smile on my face. "That was nuts."

"It was crazy." Misty laughed. "How are you holding up?"

"I don't have any words for what just happened."

Miss Sara squeezed into the booth across from us, slid her hand into her shirt, and began searching for something in her bra. "Let's see." She trained her eyes on mine. "You worked twelve hours. So that's . . ."

I squirmed with discomfort. Why was this woman touching her breasts?

"Found it!" she announced as she pulled out the wad of cash.

"Oh, Miss Sara. No. You don't need to pay me. You took me in when you didn't have to. I have a place to stay and eat, so it's okay. Really."

"Honey. Cut out that nonsense. Everyone gets paid. This ain't charity—it's work."

"No, it's fine. You've done more than enough for me." I put my hands up to refuse.

"I am not doing this for you. The people need to eat. The dishes need to be washed. Someone else will call out tomorrow, and you will have to work. So here you go." She put the money on the table.

I looked at the cash, then at Miss Sara. Her smile was gentle, but her eyes were insistent. This was not a battle I needed to fight.

"Thank you," I said, and picked up the money with my pruney fingers. Pretty soon I would have my own wad of cash; I just wouldn't store it in my bra.

Immediately, a mixture of pride and relief washed over me. It was a revelation, the way that this money made me feel. I had had lots of money before, but this was mine. I had earned it.

CHAPTER 26
LUMA-LIZ

THE WEEKS TURNED to months, and as I acclimated to the rhythms of daily life in Highlands and got more comfortable as part of Miss Sara's household, I decided it was time to come clean to her.

I found her sitting on the sofa, engrossed in the evening news. I walked in and sat down next to her. I wasn't sure how she was going to take my confession, so I decided just to come right out with it.

"Miss Sara, you know that I am gay."

Miss Sara hardly took her eyes from the TV. "That's fine, honey," she said, patting my leg. "Just don't be a slut."

Tuesdays were our days off. We usually spent them reading or watching movies. One Tuesday, Miss Sara told me to put on some gym shoes and get in the car. We were going to the mountains. Now a veteran of Miss Sara's erratic driving, my stomach mercifully stayed still as the scenery flew by. It was early fall; the tips of the hills were flecked with red and gold leaves.

The parking lot was deserted as we set off on our hike, one Miss Sara preferred for its ease and numerous scenic vistas. We didn't say much as we tackled the first incline, coming quickly to a lookout. A blue haze seemed to blanket the valleys, and the slopes of the well-worn Appalachian Mountains held us close. Glancing down the trail, I watched as the back end of a black bear disappeared into the underbrush before I could even tap Miss Sara's arm to show her.

I thought about the desert. About my parents. I pushed the thoughts away.

By the time we got back to the car, our foreheads were damp, our breath audible.

"You like donuts?" Mis Sara asked, fishing the keys from her back pocket.

"Of course I like donuts."

"Okay, let's run an errand, then." She finished the thought with a wink.

Fifteen minutes later, we were careening in circles around the parking lot of a strip mall, waiting for Krispy Kreme's HOT NOW sign to blink on.

ONE AFTERNOON, LYNN, the waitress who called in sick to nurse her hangovers, asked me if I wanted to go out with her and the others, all of them just a few years older than me. At first, I declined, not wanting to drink with people I didn't know too well. Even Misty didn't hang out with Lynn and her friends.

"What, you're too good for us?" Lynn pushed back, not so playfully.

"No, that's not it."

"Then we'll pick you up after work!"

Now I know a person hasn't experienced the Appalachians until they've climbed up a mountain with a jug of moonshine and howled at the moon. Most nights, though, we would end up at a local bar, the one with the dirt floor and the cracked vinyl booths, discussing the finer points of American beer.

Apparently, my nights were starting to concern Miss Sara. After she drove us home from work one evening, we idled in the parking lot in front of her condo. I could tell she wanted to tell me something.

"Honey, you have to be careful with those girls."

"Miss Sara, don't worry, it's just harmless going out."

"Those girls are wild and reckless."

"They're not that bad."

"You know what they call Lynn?" Her voice dropped to an ominous whisper. "The juice dumpster."

I was confused as to why Miss Sara was whispering; we were in her car, no one else was around. I also didn't know what she meant. So I also whispered.

"The juice dumpster?"

"Yes."

"I don't know what that is."

"You know—the juice."

"Orange juice?"

"No, no, no, the juice from men."

"The juice from men . . . ?"

"Yes. One night, she and big Kathy had a competition as to who could, you know . . ."

My mind was in overdrive, frantically trying to piece this together, but I couldn't figure it out. *Juice dumpster, juice from men, competition.*

"Yes, they laid there and the guys lined up and, you know . . ."

I couldn't believe that prim and proper Miss Sara was telling me this.

She clucked, now back at normal volume. "I just want you to be careful. They are nice girls, but they just keep getting themselves in trouble."

By October, leaf-peeping season was in full swing, and at the Mountaineer, tourists were piling up as quickly as the leaves. For weeks, I had been getting up early, arriving at the diner around 4:30 a.m. to learn to make biscuits and gravy under the tutelage of Teen. For Teen, biscuits and gravy wasn't so much a breakfast dish as a fine art, one requiring discipline, memory, and focus. Mistakes were met with a throaty "hrmph." Success came with a stern nod. I'm not sure that I ever saw her smile. Teen kept that restaurant in tip-top shape, though. Even the stack of coffee filters stood up straighter when Teen was around.

One morning after a sunrise biscuit lesson, I noticed a few locals gathered around the front door. I waved them away with my hand. We didn't open for another hour; they should know better. Teen poked her head out of the kitchen, gave me a harsh glare, and marched to unlock the front door. On her way back to the stove, she flipped the coffeepots on.

I was beginning to think of myself as seasoned staff, but here was yet another lesson to be learned about life in Highlands. If a tourist or a second-home owner came to the door for a quick coffee before their early-morning hike, they could—literally—go take a hike. If a local came in before work, they were welcome. Teen didn't particularly like all of them (I'm not sure if she liked anyone), but she always let them in.

One of these locals was Little John, a man about my age who was anything but little. Typically clad in overalls and a flannel with the sleeves cut off, John looked like he had walked off the set of a movie about Appalachian stereotypes.

Not long after I started serving coffee to the firstcomers, John among them, he began coming in for lunch, too. This got Teen's attention.

"He's sweet on someone," she guessed.

I figured it was Misty. She had mentioned something about going blueberry picking with John and him trying to pick more than blueberries.

That day, a flower delivery showed up just before the dinner shift. I picked it up from the hostess stand and headed for the kitchen, assuming Miss Sara or Misty was the recipient. Glancing at the card, I absentmindedly wondered out loud, "Who is Liz?"

Misty nearly dropped the silverware she was rolling. Teen was right about Little John being sweet on someone. He was sweet on me.

Later that night, Misty and I were vacuuming and setting place mats for the next day. Miss Sara was at the register when John walked in and right past her, grinning from ear to ear.

"Hey, Liz," he cooed.

"Hey, Little John."

"You get the flowers?"

I nodded. "Thanks for those."

"I have something else to show you." That's when I noticed the pile of satin he had bunched up in his arms. Little John strode confidently over to the table next to the one I was setting and began straightening and smoothing out the fabric. Misty glanced at me with a bemused smile.

"These were my grandfather's," Little John said, stepping

away from the table so that we could see what he'd laid out.

"What the hell, Little John?" Misty screamed.

There on the table were a Ku Klux Klan hat and robe. Not just any hat and robe, apparently, but the prized family heirlooms of my admirer. Stunned, I froze.

"Get out of here!" Misty said, ushering Little John to the door.

That night, as we locked up the restaurant, I felt shaky with adrenaline. My mind seemed to only operate in questions. How did a guy like Little John get the impression I would be impressed by KKK regalia? What if he knew I was Arab? What if anyone knew I was Arab? What if my skin were darker? What if my English were bad? What if I wore a hijab? Would I have been able to live in Highlands? Would I have gotten asylum?

HALLOWEEN WAS THE busiest night of the year. The restaurant was decked out in pumpkins and sparkly orange lights; cut-out witches flew across the windows. I came to work with a few plastic cockroaches tucked into my apron, just in case there was an opportunity to prank one of the servers.

As I was prepping my dishwashing station, now a familiar and not wholly unpleasant territory, Miss Sara rushed into the kitchen. "You've been upgraded to grill and fryer tonight, College Kid." She disappeared as quickly as she had arrived.

Teen let me know what had happened. Lynn had called in sick—again. "She's laid out," Teen said, meaning Lynn was hungover. "I told Miss Sara not to pay her until after Halloween."

Teen thought Lynn was taking Miss Sara for a ride, but just a few weeks in Highlands had taught me that Miss Sara took in anyone, no matter how wounded or unreliable. No matter what their demons were. Sometimes her ministrations paid off in the form of fiercely loyal employees, and sometimes even she couldn't chip away at whatever walls they kept up. And yes, sometimes they took advantage of her kindness.

The first order came back, and I lowered a basket of fries into the grease, just as I had watched Lynn do hundreds of times. Everything after that was a blur. Flipping burgers and dodging oil splatters. Sweat dripping down my back.

Halfway through the night, I remembered my cockroaches. The next chance I got, I placed a fake bug on one of Teen's orders. When she came back to retrieve the food and saw the cockroach, she jumped back about two feet.

"You ain't right," she said, catching her breath.

Turning back to the grill, I began to worry that Teen was mad at me. Maybe I shouldn't have messed with her. But soon she was back, this time on my side of the kitchen. "Put one on Lil's plate," she murmured, and then posted up to watch.

Lil screamed so loud the whole dining room fell quiet as most of the staff rushed into the back of the restaurant to see what had happened. Teen's lips curled up into what I'm sure was a smirk. Something resembling a smile. It was upward movement at least.

"You done good," Teen said at the end of the night. I couldn't have asked for a higher compliment. I could do more than just clean toilets, after all.

AFTER HALLOWEEN, THE tourists began to depart from Highlands, and Misty went with them. Back to Boston and a boyfriend, in search of a career. I was comfortable enough with Miss Sara to stay on by myself. I didn't have anything to go back to, and I wasn't ready yet to think about the future.

I enjoyed the monotony and relative peace of the mountains through the off-season, winter and early spring. Learning more about how to run a restaurant. Staff came and went, and Miss Sara slowly started to encourage me to think beyond the hills. I thought back to that day in Richard's office when I felt like an immigration lawyer. I ordered a few LSAT books and started sitting in a corner booth after my shifts, studying.

By the time the mountains were at their greenest the next spring, I figured it was time for me to move on, too. When I thought of friends and old classmates out in the world, finishing grad school and starting jobs, my new skills on the grill didn't seem as impressive. But I didn't want to move too far from the Highlands, from Miss Sara—what I had come to think of as my home base. I decided to move to Atlanta for its balmy weather and proximity to Miss Sara. I'd stay a year, maybe two, get some work experience, get my footing. The future was still so unclear. A week before my twenty-fourth birthday, Miss Sara drove me down from the mountains and into the city; everything I owned fit neatly in the back seat.

I hadn't heard from my family in nine months. If the Middle Eastern family is a bicycle wheel, I was the crooked spoke. I had been removed, cut out so that the wheel could keep turning.

I arrived in Atlanta a very different version of myself than the girl who had gotten off the bus just nine months before. I felt hardened in a way I hadn't known was possible. There was no more family, no more unconditional love; even real joy felt like a foreign concept. When the people I met there asked me where I was from, I told them Massachusetts.

CHAPTER 27
THE MOTIONS

I CHECKED ALL the boxes. A garden apartment with a roommate I found in Atlanta's gay newspaper. An internship at a law firm. A volunteer coach position for a girls' soccer team. A job waiting tables with coworkers who liked to party.

The Cheesecake Factory was in Buckhead, a busy and vibrant part of the city with glittering skyscrapers and blocks of bars and restaurants. A far cry from the ragtag crew of the Mountaineer, the Cheesecake Factory was staffed by young people in pressed oxford shirts, their ties tucked into their aprons. The vibe among us reminded me of high school sports: the inside jokes, the commiseration, the hijinks. During lulls, we shared plates of discounted Tex-Mex egg rolls and bistro shrimp pasta.

There I also found a tight-knit group of gay men. Some had fractured relationships with their families. Every now and then, it would come up. One of the boys had gone through conversion therapy; another was kicked out at fourteen when his dad caught him with another boy. I listened as they told their stories, making jokes to cover up the pain. I never shared my own.

After our dinner shifts, we went to Backstreet, a nearby twenty-four-hour dance club, and stayed out—spending every last dollar we had made—until our brunch shift the next day. These long days—and long nights—were a relief. The best strategy I had found to keep the past tucked away where it couldn't bother me.

In Atlanta, I felt myself changing, hardening. When old friends from Smith invited me to holidays with their families, I declined, opting instead to pick up extra shifts at the restaurant or go to the movies alone. When coworkers asked about my past, I usually said I was from Massachusetts—and quickly changed the subject. Slowly, I even stopped driving up the mountain to see Miss Sara. I didn't want to think about families, to see them gathered together in backyards and living rooms. I only wanted to think about the next dinner rush, the next night out. I had left behind all my Jordanian belongings in Detroit—my scarves, my masbahah; the family photos I kept had been long-ago shoved into forgotten books. Asylum had cut me in half; I didn't need reminders about the half I had lost.

And where I had once been defensive of my parents, I

now found myself thinking about them in ways that used to make me bristle. I recast them as villains in our family drama, selfish and stunted for not being able to accept me as I was. It was quite the departure from the days when I would stand up for them no matter what. But the alternative, it seemed, was to think of them as victims, as people who I had hurt deeply. And if that were true, the guilt would eat me alive. There was no other way.

I don't know if my parents ever emailed me back, and they had no number to reach me. Once, maybe twice—those memories seem locked away from even me now—I called home, usually after a night of drinking (some people drunk-dial exes, I drunk-dialed my family), but as soon as whoever answered heard my voice, they hung up. The silence between us stretched out like an ocean, disorienting in its vastness. The days and years blurred together. But the big events, the milestone events, stood out. I never forgot who was having a birthday or who was graduating from high school. In my mind, a phantom life played out in parties, dinners, and weddings I could imagine in vivid, tedious detail. I could hear their conversations in my head. I could hear their joy and laughter. I could see them shopping for their Eid clothes and eating platters of sweets as they visited each other.

But it wasn't a pity party. It was a mindset. A survival mechanism. I was strong, I was stoic. Bad things happened, and I got through them. It wasn't that hard.

Sometimes my coworkers complained about their difficult lives. One contemplated hiking the Appalachian Trail to "find herself." In my head, I laid into her. *Supportive parents who pay for your every whim—that's not a difficult life. You were born in a country where "finding yourself" is a legitimate pastime.* An immigrant friend remembered how hard it had been for her family their first few years in America, marveling that I was doing it on my own. *It's not that hard, anyone can do it,* I thought, disdainfully. *Hard is being killed for the person you love.* Another friend complained that she couldn't afford going to a concert, couldn't figure out what she wanted to do for work. *You have two legs and two arms, get a job.* I didn't want to commiserate with anyone. To hear about their feelings or share my own. I just wanted to get on with it.

The only time I let my guard down at all was on the phone with Taytay. I had called her the second or third time someone at home hung up on me. She didn't hang up on me. I gave her my number, and she began calling me once a month, sometimes more, explicit that she should call me and not the other way around so that she would be the one charged with the international fee. Sometimes that annoyed me.

"Taytay, I have money."

"I know, habibti, but I want to pay."

"I can afford it."

"I know," she'd insist. "Save your money for food or something else."

She worried about me so much that she had created a world where I couldn't afford a ten-dollar phone card, where every last dime went to eating. My irritation always wore off quickly, as she recited verses from the Quran or shared anecdotes about my cousins. I would tell her about the good parts of my life, my job in the law office, my leafy neighborhood, leaving out the parts about waiting tables and the parties. There was no need to talk about other things: me being gay or getting asylum, the silence with my parents. It was as if we had agreed to only talk about the sweet stuff, the stuff we could control.

More than anything, I just liked to hear her voice, soft and warm and unchanging. My grandmother had always occupied a space separate from my family or my country. She was an entire universe unto herself, with her own kind of gravity. Talking with her felt like finding solid ground.

Sometimes I thought about calling Abla or Omar, but I didn't think I could bear it if they hung up on me, too. Besides, they had my number now. If Taytay had my number, then everyone had access to it. Maybe they would reach out to me. But they didn't. Nobody did.

I WAS FINE. The worst was over. Maybe, I thought cautiously, I could even start eating Middle Eastern food again.

Every day on my way to work the dinner shift, I would

pass Cedars, an all-you-can-eat Lebanese buffet. When I finally wandered inside, I was amused to see a miniature Lebanon, re-created in artificial trees and trellises of grapevines. Paintings of Beirut hung on the walls, and authentic Middle Eastern music wafted softly through the dining room—the real stuff, the singers Taytay used to listen to: Umm Kulthum and Fairouz. The buffet steamed with foods most Americans could recognize—falafel, shawarma—but the menu was full of dishes from my childhood: shakriyeh, freekeh, and bamieh. I ordered in English, but the waitstaff recognized the Syrian accent I had inherited from my mother. From then on, I became a bit of a regular at Cedars, even making special off-menu orders for atayef, the traditional Ramadan treats I could keep in my freezer until the monthlong fast, when I ate one, or sometimes two, a night.

One day, I asked the waiter if the chef could make me kibbeh labanieh, the dumplings my grandmother and I used to make together, the ones I could never get right. I half smiled as I remembered my awkward batons of duu do that Taytay always presented on the platter next to her perfectly round kibbeh.

After the server set the dish in front of me, I unwrapped my silverware, placed the napkin on my lap, and used the side of my spoon to break the delicate shell of cracked wheat. As I brought the bite to my mouth, the aroma collided with the back of my tongue—allspice, yogurt, garlic—the memories of Taytay, of afternoons standing next to her at the kitchen counter, flooded my body. We were in the market; we were eating sour plums in her steamy Mercedes. I could feel her arm against mine. It was as if those memories had followed me into the restaurant, plotting their ambush from a dark corner. My throat closed, the spoon crashed to the plate, and tears rolled down my face. Moments later, the waiter returned. He looked as surprised as I was.

"Is everything okay?" he asked, gesturing to the untouched food.

"Everything's fine. I need the check," I said, keeping my eyes down.

"Are you sure—"

"Yes. Just the check, please."

I drove to work, tied on my apron, and buried the experience in the satisfying numbness of the dinner rush.

CHAPTER 28
GUILTY BY ASSOCIATION

TAYTAY WAS THE first to call me on the morning of September 11.

"They are not Muslims," she said. "Muslims don't kill the elderly, women, or children."

I knew she was referencing the Quran. But I was confused. It was early; I had worked late.

"What are you talking about?"

"Turn on the TV, habibti."

I watched in disbelief as the planes slammed into the buildings over and over again.

"They are not Muslim," my grandmother repeated. "Please don't go out."

I tried to tell her it would be okay. But I wasn't so sure it would be. Over the next few days, I watched anti-Muslim rhetoric seep into the national dialogue and into candlelight vigils. At a gas station, I stood quietly as an Indian cashier refused to serve a woman wearing a hijab. "We don't want people like you here," he said.

I was both relieved and embarrassed by my ability to pass as white.

My grandmother called daily. She asked if the FBI had come to see me. They had visited my cousin in Boston.

"Taytay, I am okay. No one can tell I am Arab or Muslim," I reassured her. I didn't tell her how ashamed that made me feel. "I am beidah," I joked, using the Arabic word for white.

"You are a delicious beidah," she joked back, using the word's other meaning: I was a delicious egg.

"And aren't you glad I don't wear a hijab?" I teased.

In my social circles, friends who used to go by Mohammed now went by Mo; Saeed changed to Sam.

Months later, when I traveled to Massachusetts to visit Misty, I was pulled aside twice for "random checks" at the airport. For obvious reasons, I stopped carrying the Quran my grandmother had given me. Instead—when I prayed at all—I recited prayers silently in my head.

A country song the radio played on repeat asked, *Did you feel guilty 'cause you're a survivor? In a crowded room did you feel alone?*

For a while, I hoped the outrage over the attacks would fuel change in the Middle East, that perhaps America would finally get tough on Saudi Arabia, the country that had produced the majority of the terrorists in those hijacked planes.

I thought maybe the Muslim faith itself would undergo a reformation, a coming to terms with all the ways the religion had been manipulated to suit those in power. When it became obvious that wasn't going to happen, I went on a bacon-eating binge; I visited a Christian church to listen to the prayers.

When the same country song asked, *Did you go to a church and hold hands with some strangers? Stand in line and give your own blood?* I nodded because I had. I profoundly loved my new country.

And then the War on Terror began. In 2002, I watched on TV as the United States invaded Afghanistan, on the hunt for Osama bin Laden. I felt sick and sad, just like I had when I was a little girl listening to bombs explode over Baghdad on CNN. I was transfixed and haunted by the images of hundreds of thousands of women and children pouring out of Afghanistan, leaving their homes forever. Where were they going to go? Who would take them in? It was the worst kind of déjà vu. I was reminded how deeply my body is affected by war, as if it were a recurring disease encoded into my very DNA.

On the radio, another country singer belted a very different kind of song: *We'll put a boot in your ass; it's the American way.*

CHAPTER 29
REUNIONS

A COUPLE OF years passed. I spun my wheels. I left the law firm after a custody case involving an undocumented mother and a father who was a known white supremacist. When the man won custody in mediation—by agreeing not to report his ex-wife's immigration status—I knew my time in law was finished. For a few months, I did some freelance graphic design work; I took and quickly quit a job at a non-profit. I continued waiting tables, kept frittering away my tips. I couldn't find an anchor.

Besides Taytay, I hadn't spoken to my family in four years. I almost never let myself think of them, but they were always there, in the shadowy periphery of my mind. What I wanted more than anything—more than money or even my own happiness—was to prove to them that I could make something of myself. If I couldn't be the perfect daughter by being straight, then I would force them to acknowledge and be proud of my career. I would build myself up from nothing, just like my grandfather, and show them that I could afford whatever I wanted. If freedom was something they couldn't understand, then I would speak a language they understood: money. I knew that when my brothers graduated from college, my dad would set them up in business, give them money for a house, just as he would have for me, just as his father did for him. That's what family does, they take care of each other. I decided that to succeed without them—without using the name Mufleh—would be the ultimate success, proof that I had done the right thing. That I didn't need a family. Not theirs, not Miss Sara's, not Misty's. I didn't need anybody. I could do it all on my own.

The most logical thing to do, it seemed, was to take the experience I had at the Mountaineer and the Cheesecake Factory—and my grandmother's stove—and open up a café. I wrote up a business plan and started passing it around to investors, mainly parents of the girls I was coaching or classmates from Smith. I shopped around for spaces, eventually settling on an old garage in the business district. Oil stains marred the floor, and every hour or so, a train rumbled by on the tracks out front. But I saw potential in the building, with its exposed beams and excess of natural light. In many ways the café took on a heavy symbolism: it was to be the culmination of my struggle to get to this new country as well as my contribution to it.

I imagined my dad looking on proudly as I did the work. "This is what's important," he'd say with a nod, "learning how to do everything on your own. From the ground up."

I buried myself in perfecting every detail of the café. With everything, I was careful. I chose the paint colors and stayed up until the early hours applying coat after coat myself. I hung paintings by local artists and light fixtures that looked like fat, fluffy clouds. Morrissey, Death Cab for Cutie, and The Lemonheads crooned from the speakers. I designed the menu to be a buffet of my life thus far: my favorite sandwich from Massachusetts (turkey, cheddar, and cranberry sauce), my favorite dressing from the Mountaineer (Miss Sara's coveted sweet Vidalia onion), and cumin-flavored lentil soup like Taytay used to make. And I refused to sell alcohol.

I called the café Ashton's after a friend's dog, a name I knew would earn us top billing in the yellow pages.

MY GRANDMOTHER ASKED me to be sure I would be at home one afternoon in April of 2002. She was specific about the time and told me that if anyone called, I should answer. So I shouldn't have been surprised when my mother called. It was an afternoon like all the others; the phone rang the way it always rang. One minute I was alone in Atlanta, in the reality I had created; in the next I was swept back to Jordan, into a world I had tried to bury.

"Hi, Mama," she said, as if it had been hours, not years since we had spoken. "How are you?"

"I am good, Mama," I said, trying to match her casual tone.

"I am coming to Virginia next weekend for Rasha's graduation. You want to come?"

RASHA WAS THE daughter of my mom's cousin. A funny, friendly girl when she was young. I had spent weeks with Rasha and her sisters on vacations in Europe and running around the olive groves at our family farm. We both had an insatiable love for books, and despite being four years younger than me, she could hold her own in a conversation about them. I knew Rasha looked up to me, and I was proud to have set an example for her when I left for college in the US.

I had no idea that Rasha had followed in my footsteps. No idea what kind of person she had grown up to be. Was she still whip-smart and kind like I remembered? Did she still have that sarcastic sense of humor? What was her degree in? I didn't know anything anymore about the family I was about to see in Charlottesville, despite the fact that they had been the beginning and end of my world for twenty-two years.

In the days leading up to my flight to Virginia, I felt outside of my body, a sensation I had only experienced in fight-or-flight situations: being held at gunpoint, sitting through an asylum interview. My nerves sensed danger, but my brain insisted everything was fine. I remembered my mother's steady tone of voice on the phone, the way she spoke as if this were all so normal. I tried to pretend that it was—packing my clothes, the cab to the airport. Just a normal daughter going on a normal trip to spend time with her normal family.

It was May. The air was warm and fragrant. As I stepped out of the taxi and into the covered entrance of the hotel, the automatic doors slid open, releasing a whiff of air-conditioning into the afternoon. That's when I saw my mother's face, contorted with heartache and relief. Behind her, a concierge, oblivious to the significance of this moment, tapped away on a computer.

She was slender still, blonder maybe. She looked a little older, the lines around her eyes deeper and more defined. She held out her arms and folded me up in them, her tears falling into my hair. Everything about her embrace was familiar—the softness of her shoulders, the floral scent of her perfume. She squeezed harder, and I felt her chest move with a subtle sob.

What do you have to cry about? I thought. As my mother tightened her grip around me, I stiffened like a piece of timber. She had no right to be this emotional. She had made me choose: come home to danger and possible death, or live in exile all alone. Meanwhile, *she* had chosen not to call, not to see me. Her life had gone on, while mine had been fractured. My mother was the villain, I reminded myself, and villains don't get to fall apart.

I recoiled from her embrace as the rest of the family gathered around us. I realized they had been watching from some unseen corner the whole time. Uncles, aunts, cousins opened their arms to me; no one knew what else to do. We kissed each other's cheeks politely like strangers. Not a single one had reached out in five years. Why would they? To them, I was the one who had betrayed them.

We went out for lunch to a restaurant near the hotel, where the hostess pushed tables together for the fifteen or so people in our party. How familiar it felt to be back in a group of loud, raucous Arabs, how bizarre to not know the half of what they were talking about, the new babies or in-laws, the recent vacations and last year's weddings. I kept quiet and tried to piece it all together from context clues, the CliffsNotes version of my own family. It was easy to not say much; everyone seemed scared to ask me questions, scared of the answers maybe, or to shatter the fragile peace.

It was Rasha's weekend, after all. Her graduation, her time for the spotlight; I certainly didn't want the attention. She hadn't changed—still smart and sarcastic—but even she kept her distance. Like the rest of the family, she was polite but didn't ask questions. It was a relief, in a way. I certainly didn't feel like talking about my tiny one-bedroom apartment, my already struggling café, not knowing what to do with my life.

HOURS LATER, I followed my mom to her room, where I had agreed to stay. As I put my bag down on the bed, I was jolted with a disturbing realization: It was the *only* bed. She expected us to share it. This was totally normal in our culture, which values proximity and sharing—beds, bedrooms, large meals. But as I studied the king-size bed, it seemed to shrink.

When my mother sat down and patted the space next to her, a warm anger swelled in my chest.

"Come here," she said softly, "let me hold you."

I shook my head no.

"Don't be ridiculous. Come here, habibti."

"How could you not see me?"

"We couldn't afford it."

"Mama."

"Khalas," she said. *Enough.* "Habibti, we don't need to talk about anything."

"I'm calling Taytay."

The long minutes it took to get my grandmother on the phone were strained with a tense silence. My mother stared at the carpet as I indignantly punched the many numbers it took to reach the Middle East. When Taytay answered the phone, I didn't even say hello.

"She wants me to sleep in the same bed," I said to my grandmother, but really, I suppose, to my mom. "How can we go from nothing to this? I can't do it."

Taytay sighed. "I told her that you are her child, no one leaves their child. No one." There was disappointment in my grandmother's voice. "I just don't know why your father did this," she said, confirming something I knew without knowing. That he was the one who had prevented my mom from communicating with me. He controlled my mom, my siblings, my cousins, the only one he couldn't control was my taytay. My mom couldn't have purchased a ticket or left the country without his permission. I knew that. But I didn't want to admit it, that she, too, was helpless in all of this. I was naïve in thinking that the lion could finally break free.

My father often called us "La Famiglia," a phrase he had picked up on a business trip to Italy. "You can do anything, but never go against the family," he'd say, quoting *The Godfather*. I had been disloyal and cast out. For the many years since my asylum decision, I'd felt like I was the one holding the key to the prison I lived in, but it was my father all along.

"Just let her be," my grandmother instructed. I held the receiver out so my mother could hear, too. I felt my breath return to a normal rhythm. I felt myself open to my grandmother's next words: "Forgive her—and be gentle." I'm not sure if they were for my mother, for me, or for us both.

I didn't sleep in the bed, curling up instead on the room's tiny love seat, but after that afternoon, there were no more arguments between us. Throughout the weekend, my mother asked continually, Mihtajeh shee?—if there was anything I needed.

"Clothes?"

"I have enough clothes."

"Money?"

"I don't need any money."

"Anything? Do you need anything?"

"Nothing, Mama. I am fine. Everything is fine."

Most of the time, we were quiet. We were together. Side by side at my cousin's graduation, at the celebration afterward, watching TV before bed.

This is how Arabs show their love, not by saying "I love you" over and over again, but by being physically present, by showing up. For my mother to have shown up in the United States, without my father or, presumably, his blessing, was an enormous gesture. I was still angry, still deeply hurt, but the part of myself I had kept locked away began to budge, as if it was an animal stirring out of hibernation.

Near the end of our time together, my mom let me know she intended this to be the first of many visits.

"I'm coming back next month," she said, standing in front of a half-packed suitcase. "With Baba and Inam." It was a good strategy; had she said just my father was coming, I would have balked. But my baby sister? I would have endured a visit from Assad to see Inam.

"It's been long enough," my mother insisted.

A MONTH LATER, as I hugged a seventeen-year-old Inam in the airport terminal, the amount of time that had gone by nearly took my breath away. The years I had missed. The child I left behind, the one I used to toss into the air like a volleyball, was now a young woman, more stylish and hip than I ever was. I hardly knew what to say to her.

"When did you get so tall?" I said, holding her.

"I am taller than you!"

"No way, you're still the shortest in the family."

My father nodded and stepped slightly forward, perhaps intending to hug me. I took a big step back. I couldn't. I purposely kept his presence in my blurry periphery in the car for the drive back to Decatur, where, as Middle Eastern decorum demanded, he sat up front. As we passed the familiar landmarks of my daily life, which now seemed so dreamlike, I thought to myself that maybe I could feel like my mother's daughter again, but would I ever feel like my father's? I still needed a villain.

When we got to the apartment, I helped carry all the bags inside.

"Mama, where is it?" I asked my mother when everything was unloaded.

"Where is what—" she said, realizing midsentence what I was talking about. In all our excitement and nervousness about seeing each other, we'd left behind the most important arrival from Jordan.

A few days before their flight, my mother had asked if I would like them to bring anything from Jordan. I requested only my grandmother's kibbeh labanieh and some grape leaves. The food had made it halfway around the world but was now sitting somewhere unattended in the Atlanta airport.

With Inam, I sped back to the airport, frantic with worry. What if someone had thrown it away?

We rushed into the terminal, where I approached the first person who looked like an employee that I could find. "There were a group of Arabs . . . and they left a bag . . ." I said breathlessly, before realizing it probably wasn't the best thing to say in an airport a year after 9/11. Luckily, the woman we stopped was Black. Skeptical at first, it took only a little explanation to sway her. "It had food in it. From my grandma. She sent me food."

"Oh, I *get* Grandma's food," she said. All of a sudden, my frantic and incoherent behavior made sense. Together, we located the lost bag and, for the first time in five years, I had kibbeh labanieh for dinner. It was better than I remembered.

BEING WITH INAM again was the best part of the weeks with my family. It was strange to see how close she was with our parents, affectionate in a way I couldn't fathom. She looped her arms around my mother's shoulders and sat on my father's lap in their rental apartment. Had I ever sat on his lap, I wondered? Had my brothers? Had I vilified him so much that I'd forgotten what he was really like? Seeing my parents' and Inam's open affection made me envious. I wanted that closeness with her, too. I was eager to make up for lost time.

Inam was captivated by the United States and wanted to experience all the different facets of my life in Atlanta. She came to the grocery with me, to soccer practices. She joined in scrimmages with us a few times, playing defender. As I watched her run up and down the field, I wondered what it would be like to live in the same place together again.

Alone in the car one day, she shyly peppered me with questions. "What's it like to be gay?" she asked. "How did you know?"

Her questions were a breath of fresh air, after years of pretending like nothing had happened, here she was—just asking.

"What books have you been reading?" I was surprised by her curiosity and assumed that a book had sparked it, maybe something she had found in the school library.

Inam frowned. "You know they don't let those books in. Anyway, I don't like reading books like you do. I found this stuff on the internet."

"The internet!" I laughed. "You have no idea how much I wish I had the internet growing up."

"Lana told me to read about it before I came to see you."

I felt a sharp pang of jealousy. *Lana is not supposed to be the one you go to,* I thought to myself. *It's supposed to be me.*

I answered her rapid-fire questions the best that I could.

"Do you have a girlfriend? How many have you had? Who was your first?"

"You seem very comfortable with all this! Are you sure you haven't been reading books?"

"No, I've been watching *Will and Grace*!"

"*Will and Grace*! I can't believe it's allowed in Jordan."

"It's on the internet—the government doesn't know how to control it yet. Anyway, there are ways to get around the blocks, you know."

I laughed, feeling like maybe my sister and I still had a lot in common after all.

"Why did you stop talking to us?"

Suddenly, the playful banter was over. My jaw locked. Inam studied the road. "I didn't," I said. "I would never."

I had to pull over to regain my composure. After two weeks of polite small talk and biting my tongue, I couldn't stay silent anymore. It was one thing for them to treat me badly, but quite another to make my baby sister believe I would ever willingly leave her. What had my father told the others, I wondered? Is that why they had never called?

On the morning of their flight, I finally confronted my father, sitting on the stiff sofa of the corporate short-term rental they had been staying in.

"Why did you lie to Inam?"

My father looked surprised. "We didn't."

"You did. You know that I'm gay. Why didn't you tell her what *you* did? Send the FBI after me? Not let Mama talk to me?" I was yelling and crying at once, losing my grip on the hardened exterior I had spent so much time perfecting.

My father looked wounded, but he did not relent. "What *I* did? Look at what *you* did to your family."

"Hassan," my mother whispered, pleading with her eyes for him to stop.

"We aren't going to discuss this anymore," he said, "not in front of your sister."

"Yes. We are. We are going to discuss it in front of Mama and Inam so you don't lie to them anymore." I felt brazen, angry, and distraught. "You disowned me. What kind of father does this to his daughter?"

"You left *us*. What kind of daughter does this to her family?" my father boomed.

"Does what? What did I do?" I screamed.

"The way you live. The way you are."

He couldn't even say it.

My sister sat on the floor with her arms around her knees, watching. Looking like she didn't recognize me. Where we were from, a child did not raise their voice at their parents—never—not at eleven or eighteen or twenty-seven. I could see the closeness of the last few weeks evaporate from her face. That's when I realized that yelling at my father didn't actually feel good. It wasn't the catharsis I thought I wanted. And it certainly wasn't the cure to the pain we all felt.

Looking around the room—at my mother's tearstained face, my father's furrowed brow, my sister's pained expression—I realized that nothing was going to fix us. At least not anytime soon. Not one visit, not one crazy shopping spree or one explosive yelling match. Nothing could put things back to the way they were before. But I didn't want things to be how they were before—secrets and lies, silence and separations, good guys and bad guys—I wanted things to be better. And to get there, we would have to start from here.

I took a deep breath and picked up my keys. "You're going to miss your flight if we don't leave now."

CHAPTER 30
AN ENDING, A BEGINNING

IN 2002, WHEN my aunt Abla died of cancer, I used my old magic for pushing down feelings—the ones that grieved my childhood hero, the ones that raged against missing the funeral—and applied that pain in a constructive way: to comfort my grandmother.

I called Taytay a couple times a week, hoping to cheer her up even slightly. But it was no use; she was devastated. Her voice on the phone was faraway and weak. And then she got sick, too. At first, it seemed normal that Taytay didn't feel well, a symptom of her immense grief—she had buried her baby—but the doctors thought it was something else. Cancer.

It was my mother who called to tell me Taytay wasn't just in mourning; she was seriously ill. The doctors in Jordan couldn't quite figure out what was going on, so the plan was to get her to the Mayo Clinic in Texas. It had been two months since Abla had passed, leaving behind her three young children.

I told my mother I would meet them in Houston and waited for the go-ahead to buy a plane ticket. Weeks went by with word of "maybe next week" or "maybe tomorrow." I waited, hopeful. I wished the circumstances were different, but I was finally going to see my grandmother again. To bury myself in her embrace and to take care of her, the way she had taken care of me when I needed it the most.

And then one morning an instant message popped up on the computer from some random cousin. "Taytay died," it said. "Allah yarhamha." *May God rest her soul.* I called my mom, but it was no use; neither of us could speak.

Without thinking, I walked into the bathroom. I turned on the faucet. I said bismillah, and then my muscle memory took over. My left hand washed my right three times, to the wrist and in between the fingers. My right hand did the same to the left. With my cupped right hand, I put water into my mouth and spit it out, and again twice more. I inhaled water into my nose three times. I rinsed my right arm to the elbow, then the left. Everything in threes. I washed my head, my ears, my feet, as if I had done it every day. Only I hadn't. I hadn't cleansed myself for prayer in almost a decade, but it came back, the instinct needle-sharp. I took the bath mat into my room.

"Allahu Akbar," I said, raising my hands to my ears. I

placed my right hand over my left and began reciting the first chapter of the Quran. I was facing Mecca for the first time since I had been in the United States.

I bowed, stood up—and then my knees buckled as I placed my forehead on the mat. I let myself cry; I sobbed uncontrollably for the first time in years. "Taytay, weinek? Where are you?" I pleaded. "Why? Why now? I was supposed to see you. Weinek, Taytay?"

For two days, I lay in bed, unable to move. The tightening had begun in my back and then spread through my arms and legs. It was like every muscle in my body had tensed up to try to refuse the shock. It hurt to walk, to breathe, to eat. I was heartbroken.

I stared at the ceiling, marking time as my family moved through the grieving process far away in Jordan. I knew Taytay's body would have been buried within twenty-four hours, according to Islamic tradition, her body placed in the ground above my grandfather's and my aunt Abla's— even in death there is no escaping the Middle Eastern family. In the three days that followed, I imagined the friends and relatives who arrived in a steady stream to our home in Amman, to mourn with my mother. How I wished someone—anyone—would knock on my door to mourn with me. But I was alone, and because I rarely spoke of my family, not even those I told could understand how seismic this loss was for me.

Without family, without even the soothing ceremonies of bereavement, I floundered. When my body began to work again, I felt driven from my apartment, like I needed to go find something. I drove to an Atlanta cemetery, searching for some monument of grief that I could pin my sadness on to. I watched from a distance as a family I didn't know lowered a loved one into the ground.

ALMOST TWO YEARS later, in the spring of 2004, I was still consumed by that sadness—still trying to make the café work despite a balance sheet always in the red, still single, still wondering if this had all been worth it—as I walked the aisles of the Middle Eastern grocery store I visited every two weeks, shopping for food that might make me feel closer to Taytay. On the way home, I drove with the windows down, inviting in the mild spring air. Suddenly, the sweet, soapy smell of wisteria filled the car, and for a moment, I was back in Amman, back at Taytay's house, the afternoon sun shining through the purple flowers that tapped at the windows. Lost in this daydream, I missed my turn and ended up on an unfamiliar street. A Buddhist temple appeared and then a simple white mosque.

Oh great, I thought, *she's leading me back to the mosque.* I half rolled my eyes at the idea.

I pulled into an apartment complex to turn around, and

that's when I saw them—about half a dozen boys, most of them barefoot, passing around a raggedy soccer ball with two rocks set up for a goal. The sight evoked vivid memories of the pickup game at the mukhayam, the one my grandmother had insisted I join despite my hesitation and my fear.

This time, I felt no hesitation, no fear. In a few moments, I would take the key out of the ignition. I would grab a soccer ball from a coaching bag I kept in the trunk. I would walk over to those boys, and I would ask to join their game. They wouldn't be too keen on the idea, except that the ball in my hands was so shiny and new, it was irresistible.

A week later, I would go back to that parking lot to find the boys again, to feel that feeling again, the one I had always felt on a pitch, on a field, on a court. Present. Powerful. Alive. Soon I would learn that all those boys were just like me—making their way in a new country because their old one was no longer safe. Boys from Afghanistan, Sudan, Liberia.

A few months later, I would start a soccer team—the Fugees—and we would go on to raise eyebrows in the white, suburban spaces we played in, but we would also go on to win championships. Months and months later, it would become clear to me that those boys needed more than just soccer, and their families needed more than just extracurriculars. It would become clear to me that I needed more, too. Not just some superficial version of the American dream, but real, authentic connection to people who felt like home. I would close the café, declare bankruptcy, feel terrified about what might happen next.

What would happen next is that I would found an organization called the Fugees Family, a nonprofit that would serve refugee families in our community. I would grow close with many of the families, including one from Syria, who would invite me over for kibbeh labanieh and tea and hours of stories all told in Arabic.

Three years later, we would open our first school, not too far from that parking lot, where children of war and famine and humanitarian crises would find a place to recover and belong, to make up for the education and parts of their childhood that had been taken away from them. And every year, there would be an international night, where foods from all around the world—the ones I used to trade in elementary school—would line a big folding table surrounded by a chosen community. By that time, the pretty sophomore with the curly hair, the one who had rejected me the night before my college graduation, would be back in my life. We would get engaged, and we would get married on a sunny afternoon in Palm Springs beneath a chuppah held aloft by Dee-Ann and Misty.

But I didn't know any of that while I sat in the car that afternoon. All I knew for sure was that my grandmother had not led me to the mosque. She had led me here.

EPILOGUE
FOR LEILA (AND ZEINA AND YAZAN)

YOU KNOW THIS part. You know that story, the boys in the parking lot. Well, not *those* boys, but the ones who came after, the ones who came to see you in the hospital when you were born, who come to your birthday parties, who will chaperone your first dates, who will be there at your wedding. The men and women who show up at our house calling me Coach, telling you the stories of our early days, back when they were eleven or twelve, and what a tough, mean coach I was.

You know the Fugees. The soccer team I formed with those boys in the parking lot, who I soon learned were refugees like me. Trying to start new lives in a foreign place after they had lost everything just because of who they were or where they lived. You know how the team slowly became a school and then a family like no other.

Maybe until now you didn't know why I was so compelled to join that game of soccer, or why I made sure to come back a couple days later. I created a place for them to belong because *I* needed a place to belong. They were me. It took me a while to understand that.

So much happened between that pickup game in the parking lot and that Saturday morning on the kitchen floor when you finally met your jiddo. The Fugees, Mommy's and my wedding, moving across the country to our new house with the garden you helped to seed. But those two moments share a through line; they were moments when I realized that I had to act, that it was my responsibility to make things better. When I met those boys, something shifted in my heart. When you asked to talk to Jiddo, another door opened that I had thought was shut forever.

For a long time, I was scared to tell you these parts of my story. The hard and sad parts, the messy parts, the times when there were not good or bad guys, no right or wrong, just real, hard life. I was worried you would think Taytay and Jiddo weren't good parents—there were moments when I thought the same, but that was selfish. They couldn't change the culture that had molded them any more than I could change who I was attracted to. Many people might not think this, but your grandparents are progressive, because to be progressive is to make progress, and they have done just that. They have made enormous steps in accepting me and the family I have created, pushing on and questioning what they had been taught to believe. To love you like they love all their grandchildren (and maybe a little more). For many years, they loved me the best way they knew how. When that didn't work, they changed. Most good things take time, and forgiveness is no exception. And as much as I have forgiven your grandparents, I hope that they have forgiven me.

Do you remember that day you cried about what had happened to me? You said Jordan was not a kind place and that your grandfather should never have said that I wasn't his daughter. You said if only he could go to a Pride parade, he would learn how to love everyone. I told you I was so thankful for these things now if only because they brought me to you. But suffering also changed me. Being scared, being alone, being poor—they made me see the world in a different way. They lit up the dark places where suffering happens, and they emboldened me to walk into those places to help.

It would have been easy for my grandmother to enjoy her fortunate life in Amman and try to forget about the pain of leaving Syria. Like almost everyone else, she could have ignored the uncomfortable knowledge that the refugee camp even existed, that thousands of forgotten people were marooned out in the desert. After all, she didn't know them, not personally, and the whole thing really didn't have anything to do with her. But instead, Taytay felt compelled to drive there, to sit with those people. To simply see them. She knew it was the very least she could do.

And then she passed along that story and that knowledge to me. I was young, and it made me sad. Some parts of my story might make you sad, but I hope they also help you understand where I came from—and where you come from, too. Like Taytay, like Jiddo Suheil, like *my* mama, the past never really went away. It lingered on in our bodies. It asked us questions during sleepless nights: *How did you get so lucky? Why are you alive when so many others are dead?* Sometimes survivor's guilt feels like an incurable disease.

For so much of my life, I felt scared or unable to tell my story. In Jordan, I could never say out loud what was inside of me. When I applied for asylum, I had to tell my story in a very specific way, a black-and-white way that left out so much of the nuance of my experience. When people asked questions about my life, I answered simply: I came to college and stayed, in a tone (the one you know very well) that there was nothing else to discuss. For years after, I avoided telling my story because it was difficult for me, and I thought it was better tucked away, where it couldn't hurt me anymore.

But now I know that it's the untold stories that hurt the most. In the open, in the light, the stories of our suffering connect us to one another and create opportunities for us to heal. Maybe this story will help other kids who feel alone and are struggling with their identity. Maybe it will help parents whose children didn't turn out like they planned. Maybe it can even help the millions of people who have had to leave their homes, to remind them that there is something strong and resilient inside of them, no matter how far they are forced to run.

As you grow up, you will struggle and you will write your *own* story. If you are very lucky, your struggle and your story will help other people, but only if you are brave enough to tell it out loud.

Don't get me wrong. I would do anything to keep you from ever suffering. But when you do suffer, I will be right there beside you, eager to meet the stronger, kinder, better version of you that comes from it.

A couple of weeks after you were born, I was rocking you back to sleep in the middle of the night. Not since Taytay died had I let myself cry so hard. Holding you and smelling your sweet head, the moonlight draped across us, I was overcome with the knowledge that there was nothing you could do that would ever, ever make me leave you or love you any less (well, maybe if you became an Arsenal fan). And you will *always* be my daughter.

It was the second revelation in the days after you arrived on Earth. The first happened in the recovery room at the hospital, as your mother and I stared at your perfect face in utter disbelief that you were ours. Suddenly, three Fugees appeared in the doorway. They had planned to ride their bikes the twelve miles into downtown Atlanta to meet you, but luckily they had gotten a ride.

They brought gifts. They doted on you. They loved your Arabic name. And sitting there with them, your mommy, and you, I realized that for the first time, my life was no longer defined by what was wrong or what was missing. I wasn't waiting for a phone to ring or for anyone else to show up. Everything I needed was right there in that room. For so long, I had believed that I would always be alone, my walls becoming impenetrable over the years. Your mom made those first few cracks, and when you came roaring into the world, you shattered it into a million pieces.

You might be surprised to hear that, because some days you have to tell me to put my work away, to get off my phone. You get upset if I miss an event at your school or if I'm lost in my own thoughts about the wars or the injustices of this world. But it's because of you that I feel even more committed to making the world a better place; I want all kids to have every opportunity that you do.

A year or so before Yazan was born, a close friend asked if we were going to have third baby. We were overwhelmed with work and two children under three; we were unsure. And he said, "Don't think about what your life looks like now, think about what you want your dinner table to look like in twenty-five years." Here is what I imagined:

There were the three of you, together with your significant others, friends, college roommates. There were families brand-new to the United States, too, celebrating

Thanksgiving for the very first time. There were Fugees who had been in our life for over four decades. Your mommy's family, Nana and Papa. My sisters from Smith—and my real sister, and her family, too. Your Taytay and Jiddo. Neighbors who needed a place to go. Gay teenagers not welcome at their family celebrations. And our table was brimming with every food from every country and culture: a turkey and stuffing, tibs, mantu, fufu, spicy noodles, and the kibbeh labanieh you and I had made together.

At some point you will experience heartache and heartbreak, and it will be the people at your dinner table who will get you through it. If I have taught you anything, I hope it is to know when to accept the hands that are held out to help you, and when to hold out your own.

Inti albi, rohi, ayouni.

Mama

ACKNOWLEDGMENTS

I AM THANKFUL beyond measure to Laurene Powell Jobs and the amazing team at Emerson Collective. Anne Marie Burgoyne and Amy Low, your unwavering support and encouragement brought this as well as many other passion projects to fruition.

Thank you to my incredible agent, Todd Shuster, for your steady guidance and matchmaking skills. Without you and Lauren Sharp, I never would have met Ashley Stimpson, collaborator extraordinaire. You are the perfect blend of Yoda, Chewbacca, and Obi-Wan. You literally gave birth to this book. Diane, Nigel, and Jeff, you are the unsung heroes; thank you for sharing this extraordinary human with me.

Thank you to my editor, Stacey Barney, whose thoughtful support and insight helped see this book to completion. Caitlin Tutterow, I am grateful for all your work behind the scenes and gentle nudges to turn everything in. Nancy Paulsen, thank you for leading this incredible team and welcoming me into your "house."

Rasha Shaath and Hana Malhas, thank you for reading the drafts and giving valuable insight and feedback. Your encouragement is what made this possible.

Thanks to the countless friends and colleagues who made this possible, I know I will forget a few: Shola, Asha, Eason, Diana, Marni, Erica, Matt, Mac, Celeste, Felicity, Anita, William, Kavita, Raphael, Bev, Jason, Aleesha, Meg, Kathy, Gary, Bouran, and Kevin.

Samanyu Chaudry and Anyaddis Ferguson, you rock.

Dee-Ann, Misty, Amanda, Sheherezade, Allison, and Chelsea, it's not lost on me how much we have been through and what you have given. Thank you for always picking up the pieces and putting me back together again.

Mama and Baba, I know this is not the life you had imagined for me. I am who I am because of you, and for that I am eternally grateful. I appreciate you and I love you.

I am grateful to my brothers, Ali and Saeed, and to my cousins (too many to name, but especially Lana, Omar, Seema, Nadine, Sarah, Laila, and Fares).

Hassan, Yasmina, Nour, and Talia, you all insisted I thank you in my book, so here it is.

And to all the Fugees (you know who you are), thank you for welcoming me into your homes, sharing your food, teaching me to be proud of who I am, and making me realize how strong I am because of my experience.

And Noura, you are too young to know this, but thank you for bringing the entire family back together for a family reunion twenty-six years in the making.

To my sister, Inam: I know you don't read half the stuff I send you, but I hope that this book does what you say it will—"help families like ours who have struggled and help them understand a little more."

And last but not least, thank you to my wife, Emily, for your incredible heart and invaluable support. Little did you know what you were getting into when you said "I do."

Leila, Zeina, and Yazan, thank you for dancing, farting, and keeping my ego in check.

To all of you: Shukran, shukran, shukran.